Market Technique

NUMBER ONE

by

RICHARD D. WYCKOFF

*Containing the principal articles, editorials, and correspondence
originally published in the magazine Stock Market Technique
from March 1932 to July 1933, inclusive*

PUBLISHED BY THE AUTHOR
ONE WALL STREET
NEW YORK

Originally published in 1933
by Richard D. Wyckoff

Second printing, 1990
Third printing, 2004

Library of Congress Catalog Card Number: 85-80545
ISBN: 0-87034-070-0

Cover design by David E. Robinson

TABLE OF CONTENTS

Flashes

LOOK for your money where you lost it.

Losses are punishment for bad judgment.

Are you riding a dead horse? Get off and get on a live one.

When in doubt, stay out. If you are in, and grow doubtful, get out.

If insiders traded like outsiders the insiders would soon be outsiders.

The moment your diagnosis is completed it becomes a command to trade.

Would you step into the ring with Gene Tunney without taking a boxing lesson?

A stop-order a few points away is insurance against a large loss in case you are wrong.

Do not operate for the sake of making trades, but only for the purpose of making money.

How to have lots of money with which to buy bargains in slumps and depressions: Sell out in booms.

The only fundamental factor that really counts in the stock market is The Law of Supply and Demand.

How much could you have saved in the past few years if you had known how to limit your risk and when to sell out?

When you realize that you are not beating the game you have prepared the way for your first step in learning how to beat it.

It is better to be out of the market for a week or a month than to make one wrong trade. Stay out and your judgment will clarify.

Successful trading depends on a systematic control of losses and the securing of profits in excess of those losses.

An investment position is a great handicap when you are trying to convince yourself that the money is on the short side.

Most men make money in their own business and lose it in some other fellow's. Why not make stock trading *your* business?

When asked whether the market was going up or down, the late J. P. Morgan replied: "Young man, I think the market is going to fluctuate."

Livermore once said to me: "I go long or short as close as I can to the danger point, and if the danger becomes real I close out and take a small loss."

How many battles would General Grant have won had he planned them with as little precision as most people use in their stock market operations?

Let us be men. If we have losses in stocks, let us admit that it is because we didn't play the game right. Why? Because we didn't know the game.

Beethoven's Sonatas are in any piano if you just happen to hit the right notes, and there is big money in Wall Street for anyone who learns how to play the market.

The place to study the market is at home after business hours. All you need is your evening newspaper. But do not read the financial news — only prices and volumes.

Dividends are all right as far as they go, if, as and when they are declared. But there are ways in which the stock market can be made to pay far more dollars in profits than in dividends.

How to avoid fifty and hundred point losses in stocks: Limit your risk to two or three points by using stop orders. But first learn how, when and where to place stop orders.

I'm looking for a man with an itch. His must be an itch for money-making. He must be dissatisfied with his present financial condition, and he must desire to remedy it.

After looking over a fine collection of low-priced and doubtful certificates, the broker said to him: "You do not need a safe deposit box. Get a kennel and keep these pups in your back yard."

You can learn to profit by the great swings in prices from panic levels to booms and back again if you will abandon the methods that have in the past caused you to buy in booms and sell out in panics.

Anyone who pretends he can make money by frequent trading in stocks without a complete knowledge of the technical side of the market might just as well claim that good pitching is not essential in baseball.

Three men came to Wall Street. The first always knew *what* was the best buy. The second knew *why* it was best to buy. But the third knew neither of these things; he only knew *when* to buy. He made the most money.

Successful speculation requires foresight. But most people buy stocks because they *are* earning so many dollars a share; *are* paying a $4 dividend; their companies *are* doing a good business. That is dealing with the present. The speculator must calculate what is likely to happen *in the future*.

You may be many miles from a stock broker's office, but if you can reach him by 'phone, telegraph, mail or on horseback, you can learn to operate successfully in stocks. I once met a man in the middle of the Atlantic Ocean, coming back from Europe, who said: "I live in Mexico and I receive your advices ten days after they are issued. I wire my orders to New York. Notwithstanding these handicaps, you make money for me."

A famous speculator, after making *and keeping* a big fortune in Wall Street, once said: "I have done only what other people wanted me to do. When they were determined to sell their stocks in a falling market at whatever prices they could get and clamored for buyers, I accommodated them by buying. When they were equally anxious to buy stocks at high prices, I agreeably permitted them to buy mine." — American Mercury.

Trading in Stocks is an ideal business when you know how to operate scientifically. Hours 10 to 3; 10 to 12 on Saturdays. Stay away when you like. Take long week-ends. And frequent vacations. Travel abroad for months. Go and come when you please. No overhead. No partners. No employees. *No boss.* You are in business for yourself. Bank account increases steadily after you know how. You can learn at home in your spare time.

Weber and Fields used to say: "A syndicate is a body of men entirely surrounded by money." An Investment Trust is in that position, at least when it starts. But unless the management pays proper attention to the technical position of the market, it will make the same mistakes as the average trader. No amount of money in the treasury, nor prestige of its directors will insure accurate stock market judgment. At the top of the boom, in 1929, a certain investment trust had in its employ an expert in stock market technique. When he told the management it was time to sell out all long stocks, they fired him, saying: "We are investors."

Why not let somebody else carry a stock while it is going down and while it is passing through that period of preparation for an advance? You should have it only when it is *ready* to move.

The bucket shops make money because the public takes small profits and big losses. This forces the bucket shops to take small losses and big profits. This practice has been in vogue since the first stock brokers assembled under the buttonwood tree in lower Wall Street.

The average man cannot judge which stock offers the most likely profit unless he is constantly analyzing its behavior, comparing its action with that of pivotal issues, and thoroughly understands the relative movements of all the leading stocks. Selecting the *best* opportunity simmers down to this: knowing just how, just which, and just when.

Why take your friend's tip that this is the best stock to buy? Has he compared its prospects with those of all the other hundreds of stocks listed on the Exchange? Will he come around and tell you when it is time for you to get out of that stock? Will it then be at the top of its swing? Wouldn't it be better to learn how to do all these things for yourself so that in case your friend's judgment is not 100% you can develop your own toward that point?

A Few Delightful Ways of Committing Financial Suicide:

1. **Putting a stock away and forgetting it.**
2. **Taking 3 point profits and 30 point losses.**
3. **Trading in stocks without limiting your risk.**
4. **Buying on thin margins.**
5. **Always trading on the long side.**

How the Law of
Supply and Demand Operates
in the Stock Market

JUST as an individual by his speech, action, habits and characteristics will indicate what he is intending to do and how he will act under a given set of circumstances, so the stock market indicates its future course by its own action.

In order to grasp this fact, one must understand that Wall Street is a great gathering place or receptacle for thousands of news items, rumors, tips, guesses and hunches, which are scattered abroad by news-tickers, news-slips, newspapers, brokers' market letters, telephone, telegraph and word of mouth.

All of these influences affect traders and investors; some only to the point where a favorable or unfavorable attitude is formed toward the stock market or a certain stock. Others are thereby induced to give orders to buy or sell stocks.

In taking this step, that is, the actual buying or selling, every individual thus registers on the tape his hopes for a profit; his ambitions, desires, or his fear of loss. When he buys a certain number of shares of stock, his purchase plays its small part in influencing the price of that stock toward higher levels. And when he sells, to just that extent he depresses the price of the stock he is selling.

If he deals in lots of 5,000 or 10,000 shares, he makes quite an impression; that is, he adds considerably to the demand or the lifting power of that stock, and his purchase may be the means of advancing its price $1, $2, or $3 per share, depending upon the resistance met in the quantity for sale at that level. If, however, he is a hundred share trader or investor, the upward impulse which his purchase gives to the price of that stock will be small. Should he be an odd lot buyer, he will not make any impression until the odd lot house which sold him the ten or twenty shares is obliged to balance its position by purchasing one hundred shares or more; then the lifting power of his odd lot appears on the tape.

If his operations be on the selling side, his 10, 100 or 10,000 shares will have a depressing effect on the price, not only according to the quantity of stock which he is selling, but depending to a large degree upon how much demand there is for this stock at the time he makes the sale. If his offerings encounter what is known as a thin market, that is, very little demand within a certain radius, and his broker has been instructed to sell a thousand shares at the market, the price might recede from a half point to three points before he is able to find buyers who will take the stock off his hands. If, however, there is a demand for more than a thousand shares at the price at which he offers it, his broker is likely to sell it all at one price. This transaction when recorded on the tape, if it be at or very close to the last sale, would, in the case of some stocks, be interpreted as a sign of strength.

Suppose a very large operator wished to buy quickly 20,000 shares of a certain stock and comparatively few shares were offered within a range of five points above the last sale. Should there be only 10,000 or 15,000 shares to be had within that range, he would have to bid the price up perhaps six, seven or ten points in order to fill his requirements. Therefore, the demand occasioned by his buying, compared to the supply which was not sufficient to fill his order without advancing the price several points, would be read by a tape reader as an indication of strength — demand overcoming supply.

The above are very simple illustrations of how The Law of Supply and Demand operates in the stock market, but there are hundreds of different phases in judging the future course of the stock market by its own action.

This Law, applied to all stock market movements, furnishes the real solution of a problem that has baffled millions of people for the past hundred years. Even now, very few understand it or know how to apply it, but the principle is constantly at work in all the various phases of stock market movements from the little one or two point daily swings, to the weekly, monthly and yearly movements; in fact, there is continuous evidence of this Law through the entire course of the market from panic to boom, and back again.

Forecasting the Wide Swings of Auburn

WE were in a broker's office in a southern winter resort, and he was telling me about a big trader from New York who had bought 5,000 Auburn around 115.

"Auburn is now 145 and that gives him $150,000 paper profit," said he.

"Seems to me it would be a good idea to take that profit," I replied.

"But he showed me a wire from New York which said Auburn would sell at 500."

"That may be; but the technical position, and its own action right now, indicate that it will sell below 130 before it goes to 500. The stock has been very prettily distributed in the upper 140s."

"I don't see how you can tell that it is going back that far."

"I am only repeating what the stock itself tells me; when you know how to read the tape, it gives you the best kind of inside information far in advance. If it goes below 130, it will probably sell at 122, and if it does that, I expect to see it make a low of between 92 and 93."

"Impossible; why this man is one of the biggest traders in New York and he has the insiders on the 'phone every day."

"Wait and see."

Auburn dipped to 139; then to 137. I made a mental note that the next rally should be about the last in the 140s. It was. Insiders were still selling. The next stopping place on the down side was 130. A rally, then 128. Another bulge to 137. More distribution on that rally.

When it was completed, the stock went down to 123, and in the following days it crashed.

My friend told me that when Auburn hit 115 the big trader appeared to be greatly concerned, and the rumor went around the office that he had sold out his stock at an average of 110. Thus instead of a profit of $150,000, he had a loss of $25,000.

Auburn plunged down below par and finally made a low of 91½. At this point there was ample evidence of reaccumulation by insiders. The stock closed that night at 94.

Next morning there were buying orders for several thousand shares "at the market" before the opening and the initial sale was 100. Auburn went to 112, and a few days later sold at 125 again.

Note the cost of taking inside information compared with the possibilities in doing your own forecasting by means of the tape — that is, judging a stock by its own action instead of by the tips and assurances of the manipulators:

Failure to take the profit of 30 points on 5,000
    shares.................................. $150,000
Failure to make a short trade above 140 that
    could have been covered in the low 90s, at say
    50 points profit on 5,000 shares............ 250,000

Paper profit on 5,000 bought at say 95, esti-
  mated when the stock touched 125, at 30
  points profit on 5,000 shares   150,000

          Total $550,000

Trading Methods

I — Obsolete

YOU used to wake up in the morning and begin worrying about your commitments in the stock market. Before you dressed you had to learn whether your newspaper contained any important news which might affect your stocks. You almost feared to look at the paper because you were carrying too many stocks on a small margin.

You were nearly always long of stocks; you seldom, if ever, thought of going short. Perhaps you did not dare sell short.

In your first hour at the office you were only partially interested in your own business, because you knew that a little after ten your broker would call you up and your real interest in the day's proceedings would begin. When he told you the market was a little lower, your heart also sank. And when you learned that some of your stocks were off three or four points, you felt sick. If the broker told you he needed "a little more margin," you began to worry about your finances; you wondered where you would come out if you took any more money out of your business.

During the day your broker called you again frequently: "The market is not going any better for you; in fact, it is worse."

Your business bored you. All your employees annoyed you. On the way home you looked at the disgusting exhibition the market had made that day as shown in your evening newspaper, and when you got home you quarreled with your wife.

You went to a movie to try and get your mind off the market but you could not. You lay awake at night for hours worrying whether prices would go lower next day; if so, you would have to let go some of your holdings. You wondered if you had to keep on putting up more margin. Finally you sank into a troubled sleep.

II—The Modern Scientific Method

When you understand stock market science you have no concern about important developments in your morning newspaper, because the news is not a factor in your operations. You know that no one can continually interpret the news into coming stock market movements. You now observe that when the newspapers print bullish interviews by big men, the market slumps. When the news on American Telephone & Telegraph is bearish, a rise of fifteen or twenty points begins. You have entirely abandoned the idea of trying to make money out of news columns.

You have learned that all the news, rumors and other developments are embodied in the action of the market as shown on the tape of the stock ticker. You know that if J. P. Morgan & Co. sells 50,000 shares of a certain stock, it does not mean that stock will decline in price; other interests may at the same time be buying 75,000 shares, and the price will advance on the net lifting power of that buying. When you see the market weaken, you know somebody has sold considerably more stock than other people were willing to buy at that level.

Heavy liquidation without any apparent reason indicates that "somebody knows something." Maybe it is a large operator just back from Europe after learning that there is likely to be trouble in Germany; perhaps he sells 300,000 or 400,000 shares of stock. But you don't care who sells or how much. You are concerned only as to whether there is more selling power than buying power, so that you can trade on the side of the heaviest battalions.

You didn't go to your broker's office yesterday. Last night's paper showed you just how your trades stood up to that time. Last evening you went carefully over the position of a hundred leading active stocks, and decided, which five or ten of these should move soonest, fastest and farthest. And which way. You worked it all out according to definite rules. You decided then what changes you would make today in your position, or your stop orders; therefore, you know just what you are going to tell your broker.

You have learned how to judge the trend of the market and your commitments are in harmony with that trend. You decide in advance just how much you will risk on each trade, and you never make one that does not promise a profit of several times the amount you risk. When you take a position with a stop order two points away, you do so because the method indicates that this stock should yield a profit of eight, ten or fifteen points. You can tell in advance not only which way a stock is going but the probable number of points that it will advance or decline in many instances.

At certain levels you increase your line, cautiously, always with a stop order. You never do this if the market goes against you; you pyramid only when the market is moving in your favor. In other words, you have learned to trade with the other fellow's money; thus you avoid digging down in your jeans for more of your own.

On reaching your office you 'phone your broker your orders to buy or sell and exactly where you wish him to place your stop orders; also how to move these stops when the market goes in your favor so your risk is reduced, then eliminated, and a profit assured. By training your broker to handle these changes in stops, you can devote the whole day to making money in your own business, while he is carrying out your instructions and thus helping you to make money in the stock market.

You do not ask your broker for his opinion of the market because you have a very sound and definite opinion of your own. You have learned how to work this out from the action of the market. It is not what anyone has told you; it is what the market itself has told you. It is not what you think about the market. It is what you *know* about the market.

No one can induce you to act on tips, because you refuse to listen to tips. You get in right; limit your risk, and get out right — not every time, but most of the time, so that your net profits greatly exceed your losses. Knowing the big secret of success in trading, you realize how foolish you were in former years to risk such large amounts of your capital in a game which you did not then understand, but which you now understand.

You have laughed at the records of the trading you did before you learned how. You did not know how to go in at the right time, protect yourself scientifically, and close your trades when you should. Now, with your thorough understanding of Stock Market Science and Technique, you know how to turn your old methods inside out and make them win.

But there are many other things that you have learned: How to understand Tape Reading; how to define the technical position of the whole market or any individual stock; how to tell when a stock is on the springboard, ready for an immediate move of ten or fifteen points, and scores of other invaluable principles that have established you as a highly successful trader.

You are now in business for yourself in this field which offers unlimited possibilities.

Would anything induce you to go back to your old take-a-chance way of trading?

You would no more do that than you would sell your 16-cylinder Cadillac and buy a horse and buggy.

Editorial

OUR first issue seems to have met with your approval. We are glad that you find the little magazine helpful, and that you desire more information on stock market trading and related subjects.

We shall give you ideas and suggestions but we cannot give advice on the probable course of the market, or of individual stocks, because we are not in the advisory business. Nor can we furnish statistics or opinions related thereto. *We do not give or sell any form of Service.*

* * *

Many people ask: "If you know so much about the market, why do you sell a Course of Instruction?" This is the answer: A dozen years ago I was able to retire had I found a man to take my place, who could successfully guide a large clientele. Being unable to find him, I stayed at the work several years longer than I should have done. Finally my health broke down. Five years were required to regain it. Now I am well again.

But, I have been warned by my physician that too close attention to the stock market might offset what I have gained and that I should not again undertake anything so exacting. "Keep away from the tape," he says; "don't tie yourself down to any steady routine; make frequent trips to Florida, California and Europe. These will help you to retain your health and keep you from ever again getting wound up too tightly in your business." Good advice, and I am following it.

I find pleasure and satisfaction in my new profession — as physician to numerous stock market patients, most of whom were once very sick. I had the right medicine for them, and now they are enthusiastic about their cure.

Flashes

THE more statistics, the more confusion.

Of all sad words of tongue or pen
The saddest are these: I didn't know when.

The stock market is dynamite if you do not know how to deal in it.

The question is not whether you have lost money in stocks but whether you are going to persist in doing so.

If everybody had placed a stop order on stocks held and purchases made in 1929, there would have been no panic.

I have been a sucker. I have dabbled in another fellow's field without understanding it.

Why spend time keeping charts if you do not know how to make intelligent forecasts from them?

Don't think because you own a stock it can't go down much farther. Any stock can go anywhere.

We hear much about "weighted averages." Many of these should be attached to a sashweight and heaved overboard.

Embarrassing moments: When the margin clerk says you will have to put up $5,000 more to save the $10,000 you already have in.

Jim Keene wasn't licked when he lost all his millions except $30,000. He started a bear campaign in Jersey Central and made $1,500,000.

A sure way to avoid big investment losses: Once a week close out every investment that shows a loss. Keep only those which are moving in your favor.

The most perfect example of following the trend would be a monkey clinging to the back of a boa constrictor as it wriggled through the jungle.

Of all the depressions in Wall Street's history, the present is the only one that has not come to an end. Oh! Yes, it will.

If you are planning a Wall Street career, there is a path that will take you 'cross lots and save you about ten years of tortuous travelling.

Are you a tip-and-hunch trader? Thank your stars you now have a shirt on your back. If you continue, you may have to consult the column "What the men will wear" for the latest styles in barrels.

If I were to give you a tip on a stock and it made good, I would not be doing anything constructive. But if I can show you how to trade successfully without asking for *anyone's* tips, I have accomplished something worth while.

Many chart players have a way of trading on "gaps"; that is, when the price of a stock jumps over several points and leaves a blank space on the chart, they call it a gap. There may be something in this idea, but somehow it always makes me yawn.

It is a man's ego that keeps him coming back into Wall Street in spite of his losses. He will not admit to himself that he is licked. Rarely does it occur to him that while persistence is a virtue, failure to improve his method of procedure delays his final success.

According to a table compiled by Bradstreet's, incompetence is the greatest single cause of failure in business. The three causes — Incompetence, Lack of Capital and Inexperience — account for 72% of all the failures. This describes the Wall Street picture perfectly.

Trading in stocks is more than a business; it is an art, a science, a profession — whichever you choose. It demands study and concentration if one is to make a success of it. Those who make trading a sideline or a hobby should at least master the principles that govern the trend of prices and thus begin to build a permanent success.

How can you select the stock that offers the *best* opportunity if you have no definite means of measuring the approximate number of points that a hundred stocks should move, and which way? If certain issues promise a twenty to thirty point profit, why go into those that might not move at all, or which may afford only two or three points profit?

The end of 1931 recorded a great shifting of stocks from weak into strong hands. Nearly 100 corporations reported a gain of over 2,000,000 (more than 40%) in the number of stockholders. How many new stockholders this indicates for the hundreds of thousands of corporations throughout the country may be left to the imagination. These new stockholders are sowing seeds which will grow into small and large fortunes in the coming bull market.

People talk about this country going to the dogs. Just what do they mean? And which dogs? Does the land sink into the sea? Do the farms cease to produce? The railroads stop running? The buildings fall down? I often wonder what the dogs will do when they really get the United States of America. Does not the history of every Wall Street panic prove that things go from bad to worse and then from worse to better?

During the big boom, Arthur Brisbane often wrote: "Invest. Don't speculate." We presume he meant: Buy outright; not on margin. Paying for a stock in full does not make you an investor. It is your purpose — your intent when you buy a security — that classifies you. If you buy a bond solely for the safety it affords and the income it yields, and you intend to hold that bond until the date of its maturity, you are a 100% investor. The more you depart from that standard, the more of a speculator you become.

Whenever the market pops up for a rally and then reacts, many wise newspaper writers label it "profit taking." To determine that this really is the cause, they would have to ask all the sellers all over the world: Were you taking profits? Then they must calculate whether the total sales of those who were *taking profits* exceeded the combined total of those who were *taking losses, getting out even* and *selling short*. Why not say: The market reacted because at that time there were more sellers than buyers? And tell us, scribes, about those rare instances where someone takes a loss. We'd feel better.

It is impossible for anyone to attain any permanent success by attempting to interpret the news into stock market profits. Millions are trying to do this. Few think alike. The buying or selling of other millions who do not know the news may outweigh that of those who do. Why not judge the market from its own action? Thus you get a consensus of the actual buying and selling, however it is generated. For, while the news may influence opinion and sentiment, it is only the orders that are executed on the floor of the Exchange that actually influence prices. Observe which side possesses the greatest power; then go with that side, whether it be the bull or the bear.

The Public at the Crossroads

THIS is an appeal to the common sense of the American people. Its purpose is to arouse our speculating and investing public to the danger of going into another bull market without being better qualified than in the late boom and panic, when twenty million people lost one hundred billion dollars in the stock market. That is an average of only five thousand dollars each; but such a loss was, in the aggregate, sufficient to wreck this country's business, many of its banking institutions, and the personal fortunes of a majority of its citizens.

The people produced their own panic because they did not know the stock market. Will the next boom find them better qualified to trade and invest, safely and profitably? Will they have any more real knowledge at their command? Very little more. Unless the public awakens to the realization that its operating methods must be improved, we shall see a repetition of the sad story.

I call it the Wall Street game because most people look at it that way. How to play this game is really known to only a comparatively few. In the five years culminating in 1929, big and little players made mountains of money, only to have it taken away from them on the way down. A whole section of our population climbed, speculatively, up one side of the Wall Street Alps and then slid off and fell down into the valley of depression.

Such calamities will occur again and again, until the public realizes that the so-called easy money in the stock market is usually money loaned — not given — and seldom kept.

Most people are flat broke or hanging on by their eyelids, liquidating their principal where they can, living on the proceeds, or borrowing on insurance policies. That the boom and panic have resulted in a national disaster no one can deny. But that another boom and consequent speculative orgy will follow is just as certain.

What is the public going to do about it? Continue to trade on tips, rumors and subsidized ballyhoo? Find itself loaded up to the ears with stocks at the top of the next boom, not knowing when to liquidate; failing to turn paper profits into cash; then seeing them all quickly or gradually vanish? It is up to each individual to decide.

Every outsider should remember that he is a unit in an unorganized and helpless public which is cajoled into the market by all the various interests that lead and mislead it on the strength of its mass cupidity. Insiders (officers and directors), pools, large operators, floor traders and hired manipulators are arrayed against this public, which realizes few of the dangers to which it is exposed. Not their reason but their emotions lead people to plunge into ventures where the cards are stacked and marked against them.

What is anyone doing to correct this situation? Are the bankers telling their depositors never again to borrow money on stocks? Are brokers warning their clients that they had better learn before they burn? Are the advisory bureaus and stock market "experts" announcing that calamity awaits most of those who venture into this field? Do investment counsellors warn that most things labeled investments are nothing but speculations? No, we hear little on these points. People have to learn the pitfalls for themselves.

Many have made resolutions that they will have nothing more to do with the stock market, for the best of reasons — because they have been thoroughly licked. Let these same people hear that their neighbors are beginning to make money again; spread a few tips among them and they will soon be at it again.

The American people are really more intelligent than this in most of their undertakings, but the stock market blinds them to the possibilities of loss. The lure is in the Easy Money, Get-rich-quick, Profit-without-labor arguments that are so infectious in times of speculative excesses.

If you had never been in the air, would you walk up to a plane, get into the pilot's seat and attempt to take off? Would you climb the Matterhorn without a guide? Would you, the first time you put on a diver's suit, go down in search of a sunken wreck? Would you attempt to manage a submarine? All these things seem reckless. But people do worse when they trade in the stock market without any experience, with little capital, and no knowledge of the business. They take their financial lives in their hands and jump overboard in a rough sea. Is it any wonder many of them drown?

Traders in the stock market may be divided into three classes: (1) Those who are absolutely led by others; (2) Those who are influenced or guided by others, gratuitously or for brokerage and other fees; (3) Those who depend on their own judgment.

To which of these classes do you belong?

It would be well to ask yourself these questions: Do you depend on the advice of your broker or his customers' man? Has this advice been profitable to you in the net? Do you trade on tips or inside information which you receive from others? Have these yielded more profits than losses? If you base your own judgment on news, earnings, dividends, balance sheets, book values and other statistics, has the market always responded to these as you thought it would? Or if you make your commitments on the strength of somebody's curves on money rates, car-loadings, automobile output, crop reports and other business statistics, have you reason to believe that these are reliable guides?

And what has been your practice in the transactions you have made? Have you followed the time-proven and invaluable rule: Cut your losses and let your profits run? And that other vital principle in stock market operations: Always operate in harmony with the trend — have you followed that? If so, you should have been out of stocks in 1929 and either long of money or short of the market most of the time since then. But those are only a couple of the things that you should have learned before you began your Wall Street career; there are a few hundred more.

If you depend on the judgment of some other person, you are betting that he will be right. If he is right when he gets you in, he may get you out too soon, or keep you in too long. Perhaps a pool has invited you to join it. How do you know this pool was not formed at the suggestion of some insider who wants to unload on you and your associates? Or that the pool manager is not giving the pool the worst of it by putting the profitable trades in his own account and giving the pool those that show losses?

If you are following someone on the inside — a so-called big man — then you should remember that most of the big men also have been wrong on the market for the past three years and there is no certainty that they will be right or that it will be well to follow them in the next three.

It is time to consider all these things — to look back on your experiences since 1929 and see whether it really pays you to go on taking such chances. By summing up all that you have learned and comparing it with the requirements of a well-qualified and successful trader or investor in stocks, you will probably find that you are sadly deficient in experience, knowledge, practice and other requisites.

Ask yourself right now whether you really are in a position to enter, with what capital you have left, another speculative season. And whether if you do so you will not again become the victim of your own lack of knowledge and ability in this field.

Not a few intelligent, conscientious and more or less experienced people undertake the business of guiding others in their speculative and investment operations. Many unscrupulous people also are using this profession as a means of filching funds from the weak and inexperienced. From the highest to the lowest type — from those who charge thousands of dollars a year for what they claim is expert guidance down to others whose fee is one dollar per month as a lure to the uninformed, we find various grades of ability being sold at so much per year or month, or for a certain percentage of the profits.

No one realizes better than I the difficulties in stock market advisory work. The man doesn't live who can always be right. But this is a statement of fact: Not only the public but the majority of those who have undertaken to guide speculators and investors in the past three years have made a mess of it. That is, they have been wrong most of the time.

I offer this suggestion: One great service the New York Stock Exchange could do its brokerage firms and the public would be to prohibit the firms from giving advice or expressing opinions. This would throw the public on its own resources in forecasting, selecting the right securities, and buying or selling at the right time. Thus the functions of brokers and their customers' men would be restricted to supplying the facts upon which the clients' judgment might be based; executing orders and giving reports; they would have nothing to do with urging people to trade or passing along tips, rumors, inside stuff, or personal opinions.

Let us see just what one hundred percent accuracy in leading, guiding or influencing others would have called for in the past three years: It would have meant getting them out at the high levels of 1929 and putting them short of the market; covering at the bottom of the panic in

November; reselling (short) on the strong rallies, and repeating this just so often as the market gave opportunities for profit. Few, if any, bankers, brokers, customers'
men, advisory agents or investment counsellors attained
any high degree of accuracy in their advices through the
whole period of 1929–32. True, some got their people out
near top prices, but on the way down they put them back
into the market too soon and did not put them short when
they should have done so.

Summing up the situation we, therefore, must admit that
most individuals and organizations who have attempted to
guide the public have fallen down completely.

And so has the public.

The public now has practically no one to follow or to
lean upon in the coming boom and subsequent decline,
panic or depression.

That being the case, it seems to me the public should
learn how to invest or speculate scientifically and successfully; or let Wall Street alone — leave it flat — and never
go back.

To nurse the idea that because you are a successful merchant, manufacturer, physician or business man you are
qualified to take part in the vast operations which center in
Wall Street is to mislead yourself into worry, strain, nerves,
failure and break-down in health, business and fortune.
The stock market is something you must learn, just as you
originally learned your own trade, business or profession.
The foundation knowledge must be acquired; to this must
be added the technique.

Trace your record as a successful business man, for instance, and you will recall that you started as an office boy
or clerk, gradually worked up to the position of manager,
partner or officer and director. In your own line you are a
success. Could you have succeeded without long training
and practical experience? Certainly not.

Why imagine that you can hand a check to a broker, ask

his advice or tell him to buy this or that stock on the strength of some tip, rumor or hunch, and begin making money and keep on making money in this most difficult and complicated business — one in which millions fail and a comparatively few succeed?

Why is it that all the common sense which accrues from long experience in other fields seems to be laid aside when a man enters Wall Street? In his own office he will frequently turn a deaf ear to some of his most experienced assistants, but in a brokerage office he will jump at a tip whispered to him by a beardless youth acting as customers' man. If he is building an extension to his factory and putting in new machinery and equipment, he calls in the proper talent to advise in the construction, designing and all the details known as "technical." There in his office he admits that he does not know all about these other things; but in the stock market he forgets his limitations and often risks a good part of his fortune on the assurances of a voice over the telephone of a person whom he met only last Thursday and about whose judgment he knows absolutely nothing.

It is true that some people have made and kept money in spite of their lack of knowledge, but, for the vast majority of the others, I don't figure they were successful when they ran their shoestrings into topboots, if, after that, they found themselves financially barefoot. In Wall Street, or any other field, it is not what one makes but what he *keeps* that counts. If everyone who indulged in the stock market during the boom would figure up what he has left now (early May, 1932) he could calculate exactly how little he has profited, if at all.

Now if you do not know how to trade scientifically; if there is practically no one upon whom you can depend; if the people who *should* have known, who pretended that they *could* guide you successfully, have fallen down, almost to a man, are you going to repeat the precarious business of betting on tips and hunches, or leaning on some other person's judgment when you again resume your stock market activities? To do so would be a sad mistake. So this is the time to come to your own decision — whether it will pay you to go any further along the road that leads to paper profits, wild plunging, extravagant living, reckless neglect of your regular business or profession, and then — shrinking fortune, lowered income and perhaps bankruptcy, as a result of your over-indulgence in a game which you had no right to play because you didn't understand it.

You ask: How can a person learn to trade or invest in stocks? I answer: How does he learn to be a physician, lawyer, dentist or make a start in any other kind of business or profession? He begins by gathering all available information about the subject. He goes to school and college; takes a medical, legal, business or economics course. He does not jump into any field haphazard. He does not hang out a sign before he is prepared to practice.

A lady once said to Paderewski: "You are a born genius!"

"No, madame," he replied, "I was once an ordinary piano player."

Consider bridge and golf: How many bridge players there are in this country I leave to you. Every one of these players was once totally ignorant of bridge. Having become interested, each is now actuated by a desire to play the game better and better. They are learning, or have learned.

In 1931, 2,000,000 golf players paid their caddies $30,-000,000 for comfort, convenience and the ability to play a better game. These golf players paid as much more for lessons.

You too can learn, whether it is bridge, golf or the stock market.

So if you decide to continue trading and investing in stocks, why not begin at once to absorb everything available on "how"? Just as you would take a course in your chosen profession, and do the reading necessary for it, spend as much of your time as you can on this subject.

Equip yourself for participation in the great game that centers in Wall Street, to the end that you may find yourself eventually a fully qualified, successful operator, never asking anyone's opinion or advice, but depending absolutely on your own judgment.

And when you think you know, don't risk any real money proving it. Practice on paper all that you learn, for as long a time as necessary. When you do know how, you will have something that will last you all your life; that should yield an increasing amount of profit and satisfaction.

Whether you decide to learn or quit, perhaps you may some day thank me for suggesting that you do one or the other.

* * *

As Elbert Hubbard wrote: "Every man who expresses what he honestly thinks is true, is changing the Spirit of the Times. Thinkers help other people to think, for they formulate what others are thinking. No person writes or thinks alone — thought is in the air, but its expression is needed to create a tangible Spirit of the Times. The value of the thinker who writes, or a writer who thinks, or a business man who acts, is that he supplies arguments for the people and confirms all who are on his wire in their opinions, often unuttered."

Knowing How

A MINER must *understand* how dynamite works before he can *safely use it.*

A surgeon must *understand* the construction and operation of the human machine before he can *safely perform an operation.*

A lawyer must *understand* the law and its interpretation before he is competent *to draw a contract or try a case.*

A navigator must *understand* how to determine his position at all times before he is competent *to command an ocean liner.*

If you wish to be a successful trader in stocks, you should first *learn how* to conduct your operations scientifically and profitably.

Why They Bought It

I SAW B. & O. down around 36 and it was the oldest railroad in the country so I took on some shares.

When Bethlehem Steel sold at 54, I remembered that it used to sell above par, and I thought it was cheap.

I'm working for the General Electric Co. and of course I know quite a lot about the company. When it got to 33, I figured that it ought to rally a few points and give me a profit.

When N. Y. Central was 228 I made the mistake of taking the advice of a fellow who said it was surely going to 300.

I bought Auburn close to 500 because I was told the stock was cornered.

I was advised that du Pont was a stock to buy and never sell, so I applied this philosophy in September, 1929.

When stocks acted so badly I bought bonds so as to avoid speculation.

Charts and the Dow Theory

THIRTY years ago New Street was flecked with chart enthusiasts, wild-eyed and long-haired, with arms full of big charts. They could always tell you what every stock on their charts was going to do, but they never had any money. Not only did they fail to steer their courses toward fat bank accounts, but they even had difficulty in navigating the revolving doors.

At that time a person who used or even believed in charts as an aid in money-making was looked upon with an expression which plainly asked: Are you that kind of a nut? But things have changed. Not only in Wall Street but in all lines of business and almost every profession charts are being widely used. In the financial district there is scarcely an office today which does not exhibit some form of graph showing fluctuations of average prices of stocks, bonds and other fundamental factors used in determining the course of securities and business. Wall Street and the country are now chart-minded.

More than ever are charts being used in recording the movements of individual stocks. This is the best way to record market history. An increasing number of people are learning how to forecast the trend of prices by this means.

Formerly this writer was very skeptical about charts because so many people were thus misled into development of mechanical systems which did not call for judgment; these required merely blind following of definite rules, upon the appearance of certain chart formations.

But as the subject was studied more deeply, it was found that charts, when rightly used, were an *aid* to judgment as well as a means of *improving the quality* of one's judgment. The more one studies them, the more benefit can be derived from their use.

There have been times when certain statistical factors

have been used by me in combination with the action of the market as recorded on charts; however, the experience of the past few years has emphasized the value of disregarding all considerations except those which relate to price movement, volume and time. If one is endeavoring to realize profits from the principal swings in prices of stocks, it is my opinion that he should disregard fundamental as well as corporate statistics relating to the stocks in which he is trading, stick closely to a study of the *action* of the market and become deaf and blind to everything else.

I am frequently asked: Do you mean to say that you don't consider what the stock is earning or the dividend it pays? Or its prospects? Or the condition of the industry? Or any of the other factors that are generally used in forming opinions about stocks? My answer is: You can get the best results by concentrating on the action of individual stocks and the market as a whole — when you know how — because all such influences as earnings, dividends and industrial prospects are reflected in price and volume adjustments before they otherwise become apparent.

* * *

Thirty years ago Charles H. Dow called attention to the importance of studying the price movements of the stock market. These, he said, contained the sum of all available knowledge bearing on the future course of the market: "The market reflects all that the jobber knows about the condition of the textile trade; all that the banker knows about the money market; all that the best-informed president knows of his own business, together with his knowledge of all other businesses; it sees the general condition of transportation in a way that the president of no single railroad can ever see; it is better informed on crops than the farmer or even the Department of Agriculture. In fact, the market reduces to a bloodless verdict all knowledge bearing on finance, both domestic and foreign.

"The price movements, therefore," continued Dow, "represent everything everybody knows, hopes, believes and anticipates. Hence, there is no need to supplement the price movements, as some statisticians do, with elaborate compilations of commodity price index numbers, bank clearings, fluctuations in exchange or anything else. The price movements themselves reflect all these things, and therefore an understanding of all these things can be obtained directly through obtaining an understanding of the price movements of the market."

Rigid vs. Flexible Methods

AS we sat beneath the palms in a southern garden, he told me of his success in buying stocks on their investment qualities. "Of course," he agreed, "these panic times are the best for this kind of operation. It is difficult to make money when prices are high because even if you wait for the big slumps, the market is likely to keep on going down and eventually you find yourself tied up."

"Don't you ever limit your losses or trade on the short side?"

"No, I invariably take an investment position. I never sell short. Somehow I can't get myself to do that. I figure on the intrinsic value of a stock, its average earning power, its dividend rate and yield. When I can buy a stock at less than its intrinsic value, I do so. If I can buy it in an important decline, so much the better. This method makes money some of the time but, of course, it ties me up frequently."

"I would call that a very rigid method of operating, and I don't see why you use it except in panics."

"If I waited for panics my money might be idle for several years. Panics do not recur as often as in former decades. So, as I am in the business of investing for myself and others, I cannot let my capital remain idle. I admit the penalty is 'being tied up' but I don't see how I can avoid this."

"You can do so by adopting a flexible method of operating instead of your rigid procedure. First, you learn to forecast the trend of the market. Then trade with that trend. You derive a net profit from a series of transactions in which your profits exceed your losses. There is no reason why you, or any man of average intelligence, should not learn to do this. You should either learn it or revise your method of investing: buying *only* in panics and selling out completely in booms. Then your money should remain idle until the bottom of the next panic — as nearly as you can estimate it."

My friend admitted that all this was true, but, as he said, it was very hard for him, at his age, to change his ways. He was always tempted to buy when he saw what he thought were opportunities.

Inside Information

IN December 1931, Mr. Kreuger, in a speech made in Chicago, said: "I do not know of any specially weak points in our company. Our capital position has been very much improved. Last year we had $73,000,000 in debts. At the end of this year we will have about $25,000,000 and, with the exception of $2,400,000, every penny of it is in Sweden where we have arrangements with the Swedish banks. Really there is nothing in that position that worries me."

The price of Kreuger and Toll was then around 5.

This was followed by what appeared to be a personal canvass by certain insiders, its purpose being to induce buying of Kreuger and Toll stock. On increased activity and volume, the price was run up close to 9 in January. Its action gave ample indication of inside pool distribution. Volume averaged 30,000 shares per day.

The inside information was: "Buy at 6, 7, 8 and above."

The tape said, unmistakably, "Get out! The pool is unloading!"

Wall Street Fallacies

1. That You Can Put a Stock in Your Box and Forget It

WHEN a stock in your box is worth more than you paid for it, you not only cannot forget it but you insist on going around and telling everybody about it.

A stock that shows a loss never gives you an hour's peace. When the market is mentioned, you think of IT. The first thing you look at in your newspaper, or on the broker's quotation board, is IT. IT nudges your memory whatever else you are doing. Your wife kids you about IT, and reminds you of your marvelous judgment. And that little devil of a stock dances at the foot of your bed when you are trying to sleep till you mumble to yourself what a sucker you were to buy it.

A lot of people should get a kick out of this expression "put it away and forget it" — a good *swift* kick.

The Wall Street Menagerie

ASSOCIATING with our well-known friends, the Bulls and Bears, we find numerous other creatures in Wall Street. The Owl, wise looking but silent — very rare. The Flea, always hopping in and out of the market. The Porcupine, forever sticking someone. The Workhorse, meaning the Managing Partner in a brokerage house. The Parrot: he repeats the tips. The Mole that gets at the root of things. The fright-paralyzed Horse that refuses to leave the burning stable. The Shark that feeds on the poor fish. The Rabbit, so easily scared. The Bulldog that hangs on too long. The Sheep, so easily led, and the Lambs so frequently sheared. The Hog, never satisfied with his profit. The Wolf that preys upon the weak. The Ostrich that buries his head when he expects a margin call.

And then there are the Jackass and the Poor Fish. Who among us has not been one of these?

Editorial

MANY people inquire: Are you still connected with *The Magazine of Wall Street?*

My answer is: No. Although at one time I was the sole owner, now my only relationship is that of bondholder. Out of my original bondholdings of $500,000, I still have $250,000 of the 7% bonds of The Ticker Publishing Company, which owns the magazine. That publication is a brain child of mine. Naturally, I am interested in its welfare, but since 1926, I have had no part in its management, its policies or its forecasts.

The magazine you are now reading, *Stock Market Technique*, is a medium for my personal expression. Having spent forty years acquiring an understanding of the Stock Market, I see no reason for hiding this under a bushel. Properly presented, it should benefit many other people; not only those immediately within my range, but others who may be induced to realize that there is a code of enlightened procedure in the stock market, although it may not be my code.

So now I am engaged in spreading this information, and shall continue to do so for several additional years, by which time I hope to have published and otherwise made available whatever I believe will be helpful.

I am determined to aid the American public in obtaining a better run for the money it brings to Wall Street.

The Higher Development of the Dow Theory

WIDESPREAD interest in the Dow-Jones Averages is a sign that the public is beginning to study stock market action. People nowadays discuss the market, its present level, its future prospects, in terms of "the averages." Everyone has his opinion as to what "the averages" are going to do. In the recent bear market, amateur forecasters had their pet theories as to how low "the averages" should go; when the market turned upward without touching their anticipated low points they regarded it as a personal grievance. The market having thus failed them, they could not think of buying stocks. Some retained this attitude until "the averages" had nearly doubled. On the other hand, many covered their shorts near the lows and took a long position when "the averages" indicated the turning-point.

When discussing "the averages" nine out of ten refer to the Dow-Jones Averages, although there is no special potency in these as compared with averages published by the *New York Times, New York Herald-Tribune, Standard Statistics* or others. Take any group of fifty to a hundred stocks of your own selection and plot them on the same sheet as the Dow-Jones Averages and you will find little difference in their value as indicators.

There is an advantage in a study of any set of averages, for we thus begin to get away from the fallacy that making money in the stock market is a matter of getting the right tips.

Few traders actually appreciate the possibilities contained in the very essence of the Dow theory which was: "The price movement represents everything everybody knows, hopes, believes and anticipates." Dow meant that the key to the trend of the market is found in the action of the market itself. Had Dow lived, he unquestionably would have been emphasizing his principle to this day.

Some ten years ago, the late W. P. Hamilton, then Editor of the *Wall Street Journal*, wrote a book on the Dow theory about the stock market. In applying the Dow theory, Hamilton occasionally forecasted the trend of the market correctly. And while all this added somewhat to the general knowledge of the subject, Hamilton did not get very far because he did not know how.

To become a good judge of the stock market, constant study and practice are necessary. That is what Dow was doing up to the time he died. I used to see him mornings, before the market opened, walking across Broad Street from Dow Jones & Co.'s office to that of Robert Goodbody & Co. Under his arm he carried a bundle of charts, and his current writings indicated that he studied these and the tape assiduously.

At that time I was a member of a New York Stock Exchange firm, and though interested in the comparatively brief essays of Dow on Stock Market Trading Technique, I did not give these their true value until I began to publish *The Ticker*, a magazine devoted to stock market practice, predecessor of *The Magazine of Wall Street*. My subscribers required more light on judging the market by its own action. I met their requirements, and in so doing had ample opportunity to test the Dow principle; for in the years that followed — 1907 to 1926 — my researches in stock market action and my continual practice in judging the current and probable future trend of the market formed the basis for a tremendous business and a large following in financial publishing and advisory work.

Had I continued to use the Dow principle only as he developed it, I would not have gotten very far; I would probably still be following the cumbersome plan of waiting for the rails to confirm the industrials; but my work kept me at the stock ticker five hours a day and the many long years of striving to perfect my technique resulted in these, among other conclusions:

Trends. Dow stated that there were three trends to the market — long, intermediate, and day-to-day. I found that there were also hourly trends, with buying and selling waves each averaging somewhat less than a half hour. Also that these hourly trends were forecastable by means of a technique similar to that employed in judging the three others.

The technical trends of individual stocks also number four, as stated above. While the method of judging these resembles that used in forecasting the trend of the whole market (or, say, of any averages), there is a special technique which may be applied to individual issues, whether judged from the tape without any memoranda, or from charts which record market history, and which form a basis for such judgment.

Turning Points. Instead of waiting for the averages to confirm each other, perhaps far after the actual turning point, I found it possible to judge these turning points right on the nose, and was frequently able to pick the psychological hour when these should and did occur. I did not wait for the Motors to confirm the Steels, or the cats to confirm the dogs; the evidence was right there before me. While no one's judgment is 100% over a long period, I accomplished this most desirable of stock market objectives frequently enough to prove that it was not by accident but was the result of correct reasoning.

As to the turning points in individual stocks to which I have devoted much attention, it has been demonstrated that when one knows how, trading from the tape may be done with stop orders varying from $\frac{1}{4}$, $\frac{1}{2}$ to 1 point away from the danger points, and by this I do not mean a line of tops or bottoms or such formations as are frequently labelled this and that, but by a scientific method of judging supply and demand — support and pressure — using what — in the mechanical field — would be called instruments of precision.

Judging Distance. Another important adjunct in stock trading, known by very few people, is how to judge the number of points the averages or any group of stocks or any individual stock should move in a certain direction, subject to continual confirmation, correction or perhaps contradiction, as indicated by market action. Some people believe they can do this by other means, which I also understand, but I have not found these reliable, and have discarded them.

Having accomplished the above, I am able to forecast with a satisfactory percentage of accuracy the probable number of points the whole market should advance or decline; and what is of even greater value, the probable number of points individual stocks should move, and which way.

Selection of the Best Opportunities. Ability to judge distance has pointed the way to another forward step. By comparing the probable distance each stock out of a group of say one hundred should move, I have for many years past been able to decide which stocks should afford the most satisfactory profits. Without such an advantage, one is likely to get into stocks which give the poorest returns; but by choosing these live ones, the greatest profits are procurable; capital is turned over frequently, and the year's net profits greatly enhanced.

Further Developments. I am working now on what should be a further round-up of the best there is in the by-products of the Dow theory. My purpose is, in many instances, to anticipate, by minutes or hours, the top of the last bulge in an up-swing, or the last drive in a decline in the market, or in certain stocks, so that I can calculate at about what price and approximately what hour and minute these turn-ing points should occur. Thus armed, one may have his orders to buy and sell arrive at those certain trading posts on the floor of the New York Stock Exchange as near as possible to the very moment when the top or bottom price is there being recorded.

All these advantages in trading and forecasting I have derived from the Dow *principle:* "The action of the market itself is the best indication of its future course." Not from the *methods* of Dow, or Hamilton or anyone else has this been done; but by taking that principle and developing it through long years of concentration on Stock Market Technique, combined with continual practice in forecasting, trading and money-making.

The Tape Forecasted the Turn

ONE of the most important things to know about the market is whether it is in a bullish or bearish position — that is, whether the trend is upward or downward.

The same thing is desirable to know about any single stock, or group of stocks such as are represented by the averages, or, in the case of our studies, by the one hundred leading active stocks, of which we keep a record. The percentage of these hundred stocks which are in a bullish or bearish position is in itself an indication of the trend of the market.

During the last week in May 1932, nearly one hundred per cent of these stocks were in a bearish position, indicat-ing a further considerable down-swing. From that time, the percentage of stocks in a bearish position decreased rather sharply, especially those that indicated down-swings of from ten to thirty points.

The three to five point declines were, during the month of June, fluctuating between a percentage of about twenty-five to seventy-five. These short down-swings would be indicated, then they would actually occur; then, having been accomplished, there would be fewer in the short-swing bearish position, which was evidence of a lessening of the pressure.

The long down-swings were, in June, reduced in percentage to, say, from ten to thirty, whereas in May they had ranged from thirty to one hundred. Clearly, all this was the forerunner of a change in the long trend, and when, in July, the market was put to its final test, there was a constantly reduced percentage until, toward the end of the month, a mere handful of stocks were in a bearish position. On the other hand, issues in a bullish position began rapidly to run up from about ten per cent in the first week of July to as high as eighty-eight per cent for the short moves, and around thirty per cent for the long upward moves in the last week of that month.

August percentages began with strongly marked bullish indications, and with little or nothing on the bear side. A percentage of less than ten for the short down-swings and nothing at all for the long down-swings were characteristic of the first half of that month. During the latter half, an average of ten to twenty per cent indicated short down-swings which were nothing more than technical reactions. There was practically nothing on the long down-swing side.

Those able to judge the market in this way have what is probably the most farsighted barometer that exists. We find that it forecasts coming changes from one to three weeks in advance. In fact, these changes are apparent when none of the other trend charts or other indicators contain any suggestion of a change.

"It marks a big step in a man's development when he comes to realize that other men can be called in to help him do a better job than he could do alone." — *Andrew Carnegie.*

How the Technician Judges the Stock Market

A STOCK market technician's study of the market is continuous. Every hour and minute of every stock exchange day he watches its action as recorded in the transactions which appear on the tape of the stock ticker. He has certain methods of analyzing, weighing and forming conclusions from his study of the transactions, which are made up of advances, declines, rallies, reactions, etc. He closely observes the volume of the transactions, and just when the volume is light, heavy or medium, as well as the speed and momentum of the market in these various phases. While to the average observer, and those untrained in technique, there appear many miscellaneous transactions in a lot of different stocks, some active, others sluggish; some frequent, and others infrequent, everything has its meaning to the trained eye. Long experience enables him to interpret what to others appears to be a jumble of stock market events, into a very definite expression of the millions of minds whose emotions are registered on the narrow ribbon of paper by means of their actual buying and selling.

An experienced judge of the market regards the whole story that appears on the tape as though it were the expression of a single mind; that is, the composite mind of all the traders, investors, bankers, pools, institutions and others who are participating in the transactions. To illustrate: If there were ten men in a room making transactions in a stock, and not a single one of them knew what the others were doing, and if their transactions appeared on a tape, it would be possible to form an opinion of the trend of that stock as influenced by their combined transactions. Some might be selling; others buying. But if they were to trade continuously in that certain stock the evidence of its immediate course would be found in how, when and how much they actually bought and sold. Every experienced tape reader recognizes this to be a fact.

In order to realize the difficulty involved in gauging all stock market operations and especially in judging the plans and purposes of large interests by observing the action of the stocks in which they are operating, the following facts should be borne in mind: The tape of the stock ticker resembles a moving picture. The scene changes every moment. While the story is continuous, the outcome of the drama is not always clear, although the trend of events may be so to a certain degree. Just as a scenario writer endeavors to mystify his audience, so pools and manipulators strive to confuse and influence the public into thinking a stock is moving in a certain direction when the ultimate purpose is to have it move the other way.

In endeavoring to ascertain the present position of the market, the technician begins by ascertaining its present location, just as a navigator takes his bearings and sets the course of the ship. The market is always in a certain well defined position, no matter what conditions may be. It is either in a strong uptrend, or in a slow advance, or in a reaction, or a rally from a reaction, or in a recovery from a slump, or in some other position which he is able to discern and designate. At times the situation is so evenly balanced that he regards it as in a neutral position. In that case, he favors neither the long nor the short position. He waits for a definite trend before taking a full line of stocks, although he may deal in a few issues promising immediate results.

Having located his position on the market map, he sets his course in the probable direction of the next important swing. His next step is to select the stocks which should yield the greatest amount of profit in the shortest length of time. Just as the market as a whole has its technical position and probable trend, so each individual stock is in a certain technical position and has its own trend. A close study of its action enables him, in the majority of cases, to state whether it is moving in accordance with the trend of the general market or in a contrary direction. Naturally, if the trend of the general market is upward, he selects the stocks which individually are in an upward trend. In every important move in an individual stock there is a period of preparation. Just as a race horse is trained and groomed for a certain race on a given day so a stock which is to have a substantial move in a certain direction finally reaches a point in its market gyrations which is the equivalent of being ready to go. Another illustration would be that of a swimmer who steps out to the end of the spring-board. When he gets there we naturally infer that he is about to dive. How far he will go thereafter, depends upon his strength and endurance.

There are certain ways in which, in many instances, the approximate extent of a rise or decline in a stock may be determined. That is, a stock selling at 80 may give indications that it is being accumulated for a rise to 100, whereas another stock selling at 70, may hold promise of a rise to only 75. In such a case, he would naturally choose the stock which will probably yield the greater number of points profit. If this stock is being accumulated within a range of 80 to 83, he tries to buy it as near to 80 as he can, so as to reduce the risk and secure the maximum profit.

Having made his purchase, he holds his position until the objective point is reached or until he observes contradictory signs. It should be understood that large banking interests and leading pool operators cannot always carry out their plans as they are originally arranged. They may accumulate a large line of stock at the 80-83 level, intending to benefit by a probable rise to 100, but by the time the stock reaches 90, the whole financial situation or the circumstances surrounding that particular stock may have altered. Hence, it becomes advisable for them to close out their holdings and wind up the campaign.

Their operations may be spread over ten, twenty or fifty different stocks, or confined to a few, but the operating principles are the same. Any individual, pool or syndicate dealing in the stock market has only one object — to make money — and as conditions throughout the world have direct or indirect influence on the course of the stock market and on individual stocks, all campaigns are invariably undertaken with the provision that a modification or complete change in tactics may be necessary at a moment's notice.

Why Study Statistics?

YOU say you must have an economic or a statistical reason for buying and selling: Did your tabulation of Car Loadings tell you, in August 1929, that railroad traffic would decline for three years? Did your statistical manual contain any intimation that New York Central would shrink from 250 to 10? Did your Index of Business Activity tell you to cover your shorts and take a long position in July 1932? Weren't those figures still bearish?

Was there anything in the Steel Production figures that said: Buy U. S. Steel at 22, Bethlehem at 8, or Republic at 2?

And those Statements of Corporation Earnings: Did they say the turn had come? Or the Charts of Money Rates, Commodity Prices, Chain Store Sales, and other figures you watch so closely — weren't they all pessimistic and making you more and more bearish?

Honestly, now, how much dollar-benefit have you derived from all your study of the vast array of statistics in the past three years? Didn't these figures keep you long of stocks till the panic scared or squeezed you out? And didn't they get you in again too soon, or keep you bearish till long after bargain days had passed?

Then what good are they?

Why not form your conclusions from the action of the market itself? Then you will be getting your information at first hand — reliable information.

And when you know how to interpret market action, you will make far more money out of the stock market — and keep it — than if you had all the world's Fundamental Statistics poured into your lap every minute of the day. For the effect of all the Statistics that you and millions of people absorb from their daily newspapers and news tickers is all boiled down on the tape.

Flashes

IN stock trading you must have plenty of nerve but no "nerves."

Don't monkey with the stock market buzz-saw till you know how to cut wood.

God loveth a fluent and uncomplaining loser, but even the Devil detesteth a belly-acher.

He was an aviator but he couldn't get himself to take the short side of the market. It is too risky, he said.

A tip is a bit of misinformation divulged by someone who heard it from a person with whom it did not originate.

The best inside information is on the tape. I would rather follow its indications than act on a tip from J. P. Morgan himself.

For the man who does not understand scientific trading in stocks, it is much better to buy partnerships than to grab for fluctuations.

Just as the seeds of the late panic were sown in the 1929 bull market, so the roots of the August, 1932, rise were grounded in the previous depression.

Some friends of mine would be excellent judges of the stock market if they did not try to mix economics with technique. These two factors too often contradict each other.

Even if it were not true, as the Washington investigation proved, that some of the news is subsidized, it would not be possible for anyone continually to interpret the news so as to derive profits.

"What I don't like about these new electric quotation boards," said a trader, "is that when I am losing money they always seem to snicker. Naturally, I am sensitive about this."

Many who are not successful traders join pools because they think those who manage pools can trade better than they. But when they hunt deer they pull their own triggers, because they have learned how to shoot.

Legislation against corporation directors who operate pools on the long and short side of their own stocks will not help the public, for if such laws were passed we should find that aunts, cousins and grandmothers were members of the pools.

Funny how a man will stay away from a stock after it has given him a good spanking. A prominent floor trader tells me he sold 10,000 General Motors short at 82. When they rallied it to 92 he took a 10 point loss, and after losing that $100,000 he didn't have the nerve to hit it again.

The Bible names a couple of good traders who deserve mention: Jacob kept bidding up until Esau filled his bid with a mess of lentil soup. Then there was the merchant who went away and left his sons so many talents. The one who *traded* with his talents secured the greatest reward.

No security in the market today can be considered impregnable enough to put away in your vault with positive assurance that its intrinsic value and earning power will never depreciate. Conditions are constantly changing and the industries directly affecting your stocks and bonds are sensitive to these economic changes.

Most people read the tape *after* they have made a trade, in order to see how their stock is coming on. Bad practice. They should study the tape beforehand, decide when to trade, when to hold on, and when to close out. The tape will tell them all these things, if they know how to read it.

You ask: If I judge the market by its own action, as indicated on the tape, what shall I do with this vast array of statistical manuals, compilations, services and data that I have been accumulating and subscribing to for years?

My suggestion is that you pile it all up on a table, push the table up to the window, and, making sure that no one is below, tilt one end of the table.

In our Wall Street Menagerie we omitted to mention the Straddle Bug who tries to make money out of both the long and the short side of the market at the same time. Every so often one of these adepts calls to explain his marvelous method of taking money out of Wall Street. He buys one hundred shares of Union Pacific and then sneaks off down the Street and sells one hundred Union Pacific "short" through another broker. If the price declines, he takes his "profit" on the "short sale." Or, if the price advances he sells out his "long" stock. It never dawns on him that his net position is neutral, and that he has paid two commissions for which he has nothing to show. Would you believe there are people like that?

"There is a principle which cannot fail to keep men in everlasting ignorance; that principle is contempt prior to examination." — *Dr. Paley.*

Speculation as a Fine Art
By Dixon G. Watts

First of a series of articles containing some of the wisdom of famous
Wall Street operators. Mr. Watts, many years ago, was a leading
operator in cotton, and this article by him is one of the oldest on the
subject of speculation as well as a classic in its line.

ALL business is more or less speculation. The term speculation, however, is commonly restricted to business
of exceptional uncertainty. The uninitiated believe
that chance is so large a part of speculation that it is subject
to no rules, is governed by no laws. This is a serious error.
We propose to point out some of the laws in this realm.

Let us first consider the qualities essential to the equipment of a speculator. We name them: Self-reliance, judgment, courage, prudence, pliability.

1. SELF-RELIANCE: A man must think for himself, must
follow his own convictions. George Macdonald says: "A
man cannot have another man's ideas any more than he
can have another man's soul or another man's body."
Self-trust is the foundation of successful effort.

2. JUDGMENT: That equipoise; that nice adjustment of
the faculties one to the other, which is called good judgment, is an essential to the speculator.

3. COURAGE: That is, confidence to act on the decisions
of the mind. In speculation there is value in Mirabeau's
dictum: "Be bold, still be bold, always be bold."

4. PRUDENCE: The power of measuring the danger, together with a certain alertness and watchfulness, is very
important. There should be a balance of these two, prudence and courage; prudence in contemplation, courage in
execution. Lord Bacon says: "In meditation all dangers
should be seen; in execution none, unless very formidable."
Connected with these qualities, properly an outgrowth of
them, is a third, viz., promptness. The mind convinced, the
act should follow. In the words of Macbeth: "Henceforth

the very firstlings of my heart shall be the firstlings of my hand." Think, act, promptly.

5. PLIABILITY: The ability to change an opinion, the power of revision, "He who observes," says Emerson, "and observes again, is always formidable."

The qualifications named are necessary to the make-up of a speculator, but they must be in well-balanced combination.

* * *

LAWS ABSOLUTE: Never overtrade. To take an interest larger than the capital justifies is to invite disaster. With such an interest a fluctuation in the market unnerves the operator, and his judgment becomes worthless.

Never "Double up"; that is, never completely and at once reverse a position. Being long, for instance, do not sell out and go as much short. This may occasionally succeed, but is very hazardous, for should the market begin again to advance, the mind reverts to its original opinion and the speculator covers up and goes long again. Should this last change be wrong, complete demoralization ensues. The change in the original position should have been made moderately, cautiously, thus keeping the judgment clear and preserving the balance of the mind.

Run quick, or not at all; that is to say, act promptly at the first approach of danger, but failing to do this until others see the danger, hold on or close out part.

When doubtful, reduce the amount of the interest; for either the mind is not satisfied with the position taken, or the interest is too large for safety. One man told another that he could not sleep on account of his position in the market; his friend judiciously and laconically replied: "Sell down to a sleeping point."

* * *

RULES CONDITIONAL: These rules are subject to modification according to the circumstances, individuality and temperament of the operator.

It is better to "average up" than to "average down." This opinion is contrary to the one commonly held and acted upon; it being the practice to buy and on a decline to buy more. This reduces the average. Probably four times out of five this method will result in striking a reaction in the market that will prevent loss, but the fifth time, meeting with a permanently declining market, the operator loses his head and closes out, making a heavy loss — a loss so great as to bring complete demoralization, often ruin.

But buying at first moderately, and as the market advances adding slowly and cautiously to the line — this is a way of speculating that requires great care and watchfulness, for the market will often react to the point of average. Here lies the danger. Failure to close out at the point of average destroys the safety of the whole operation. Occasionally a permanently advancing market is met with and a big profit secured. In such an operation the original risk is small, the danger at no time great, and when successful the profit is large. This method should only be employed when an important advance or decline is expected, and with a moderate capital can be used with comparative safety.

To "buy down" requires a long purse and a strong nerve, and ruin often overtakes those who have both nerve and money. The stronger the nerve the more probability of staying too long. There is, however, a class of successful operators who "buy down" and hold on. They deal in relatively small amounts. Entering the market prudently with the determination of holding on for a long period, they are not disturbed by its fluctuations. They are men of good judgment, who buy in times of depression to hold for a general revival of business — an investing rather than a speculating class.

Stop losses and let profits run. If small profits are taken, then small losses must be taken. Not to have the courage to accept a loss, and to be too eager to take a profit, is fatal. It is the ruin of many.

Public opinion is not to be ignored. A strong speculative current is for the time being overwhelming, and should be closely watched. The rule is, to act cautiously with public opinion: against it, boldly. To go with the market, even when the basis is a good one, is dangerous. It may at any time turn and rend you. Every speculator knows the danger of too much "company." It is equally necessary to exercise caution in going against the market. This caution should be continued to the point of wavering — of loss of confidence — when the market should be boldly encountered to the full extent of strength, nerve and capital. The market has a pulse, on which the hand of the operator should be placed as that of the physician on the wrist of the patient. This pulse-beat must be the guide when and how to act.

In forming an opinion of the market, the element of chance ought not to be omitted. There is a doctrine of chances — Napoleon in his campaigns allowed a margin for chance — for the accidents that come in to destroy or modify the best calculation. Calculation must measure the incalculable.

It is better to act on general than special information (it is not so misleading), viz., the state of the country, the condition of the crops, manufacturers, etc. Statistics are valuable but they must be kept subordinate to a comprehensive view of the whole situation. Those who confine themselves too closely to statistics are poor guides. "There is nothing," said Canning, "so fallacious as facts, except figures."

When in doubt do nothing. Don't enter the market on half convictions; wait till the convictions are fully matured.

We have written to little purpose unless we have left the impression that the fundamental principle that lies at the base of all speculation is this: *Act so as to keep the mind clear, its judgment trustworthy*. A reserve force should therefore be maintained and kept for supreme movements, when the full strength of the whole man should be put on the stroke delivered.

It may be thought that the carrying out of these rules is difficult. As we said in the outset, the gifted man only can apply them. To the artist alone are the rules of his art valuable.

———————

There are bulls, bears and various other animals, insects and parasites in Wall Street, but the worst of all is the straddle-bug. His way of advising you always leaves him a loop-hole so that he can go back and prove to you that no matter what happened he was right.

Are you getting rich backwards? Then you are taking two points profit on your speculative trades and letting your losses run. Why not reverse this rule? Limit your risk to one, two or three points and let your profits run. But first learn how to place stop orders scientifically.

The stock market is like a moving-picture film on which every flash is different in some respect from those that precede and follow. By observing every detail that appears on a film one may study the action of the characters, read their purposes, and judge what they are likely to do when put to the test. Obviously, nothing like a cut and dried system can be applied to such a series of observations, but it is frequently possible to tell, early in a film, how the action will terminate, notwithstanding the efforts of the author to disguise his purpose and deceive his audience. So it is with manipulation as it appears on the tape.

Truly there is a tide in the affairs of men; but there is no gulf stream setting forever in one direction. — *James Russell Lowell.*

Editorial

These Foregone Conclusions

I AM NOT one of the many who form (on flimsy premises) opinions as to the future course of the stock market and then insist that the market justify their predictions.

I never try to rub the market's nose in my theories. Long ago, I learned that the market disregards what anyone thinks it should do. It has a way of its own.

It is enough to know that the market tells me what it is probably going to do *today* and in the near future. I do not expect to be informed very far in advance, because the market often changes its course. I must change my position accordingly.

Thus my mind is a slate on which the market writes its forecasts; these I accept at par. As for its instructions, these I shall execute — promptly and confidently. And when indications are altered or reversed, I shall continue to obey, because I am convinced that the market knows more than I know about its own future: more, in fact, than anybody and everybody.

Why then should I pamper my ego by theorizing and making silly predictions as to "what the market is going to do" after New Year's or the Fourth of July?

Judging the Market by Tests and Responses

MANIPULATORS are constantly testing the market to see whether it is most responsive on the bull or the bear side. They want to know whether they can get a following in the industrial, rail or utilities group, or in any other group or stock representing a certain industry.

Imagine, if you can, that the whole market is controlled by what we may call the Composite Operator, and that every move is either the result of his operations or of those influenced by him. Suppose this Composite Operator has a long position in most of the leading active stocks; this makes him desirous of advancing prices whenever he can, in order to help his whole position. He is like a general advancing into the enemy's territory. His allies are all the bulls. His enemies are all kinds of bears. His object is to defeat the bears. This he does in varying degree whenever he advances a stock.

Now suppose, at the opening of the market today, this C. O. wants to know whether the temper of the public is bullish or bearish: First he tests out the rails by advancing Union Pacific one or two points. He observes how much response is given, as indicated by advances in other rails. If none of these follows his lead upward; if the other leading rails drag themselves up a fraction and nobody operating in the rails takes the cue from the C. O. and advances others in that group, he decides that he cannot get a following in that group for the time being.

Next he tests out Can, Steel, Telephone in the same way. He gets some following in Can, a little in Telephone and nothing much in Steel. Then he tries out the utility group and gets a little more encouragement on the bull side.

From this series of tests he now knows that he can best advance the market by bulling Can. He feels out the other stocks that sometimes respond to the leadership of Can so as to get help or at least support from other sections of the market. He finds a little more response in other industrials and when he has these sized up he goes ahead and bulls the ones that show the best response — that seem most to influence the rest of the list.

Observe that he follows the line of least resistance. He avoids bulling the rails because he would there have to play a lone hand. He does not want to take big blocks of stocks which stand in his way; someone else can do that. He advances the ones that are easiest to put up while requiring the smallest purchases on his part. After a while the small bulges which he has produced in his testing operations, followed by the more active bidding up of a larger number of stocks, encourage floor traders and the public to get in on the bull side. An increasing number of stocks advance on expanding volume and a bull swing of substantial proportions is under way.

The C. O. further encourages this bullishness by helping along wherever he can. If he sees certain stocks or groups lagging, he will send a broker into those crowds to bid them up. If weakness breaks out anywhere, he will give support. As a good general he is always endeavoring to hold his lines against attack and to advance his front lines (tops) as far as he can.

Suppose the bull swing has now been running for several days and after sizing up the situation by a series of tests, he finds that the buying power has temporarily become somewhat exhausted; that is, most of the people who could be influenced to go in and buy have done so; they cannot spend that same money twice and there is a scarcity of other buyers to take their places. Demand has shrunk.

He now supplies whatever the market will take; he sells all he can around the top of the swing and on the way down. If the rise in the averages has amounted to 10 points, he may keep on selling until it has declined 6 points; then he may begin to buy back what he has sold — not by bidding up these stocks but taking them as they are offered. Out of 1,000 shares offered at a certain price he may take 600 or 700 leaving 300 still offered and the market unchanged. His reaccumulation is not apparent. The market is still heavy although he is buying back on the reaction.

After a while he absorbs most of the floating supply at a level about half way back from the top. The selling power is now lessening; in fact, he is unable to buy back all he wants; so he drives several stocks downward to weaken the market so he can complete his purchases on the reaction. These drives are also his tests. While these stocks are weak, others advance a little as a result of his raising buying limits. Thus the averages are scarcely altered. People who are bearish point to the few weak stocks and decide that the market is going much lower. They make some ventures on the short side. These help the C. O. to buy more. He takes their offerings.

With the bears making no progress and no more stock pressing for sale, the market is now in a position technically known as "sold out" for the time being. All the offerings of those who sold on the way back from the top are now absorbed; hence, for the next five points up — on the averages — there is little opposition to an advance. The C. O. therefore adds to his lines, buying as carefully as he can, so as not to advance prices.

After the averages have recovered about 3 points out of the 5 they lost, he has replaced about all the stock he wants and begins to bid up prices all around the room. The market advances to the level of the previous top. Here a lot of those who bought at that time and who held through the reaction place selling orders so they can get out even or at a small profit. This makes a lot of activity and narrow swings around the old top and chart observers say: Here is a double top; we should sell short on this. But the C. O. finds that the long selling combined with the short selling is not sufficient to stop the advance of the market. There is a latent buying power that appears to increase on advances. He bids certain stocks up to new highs in order to encourage this outside buying power.

The strength spreads to other issues and the market goes on through the old high for the averages. Bears, finding they are wrong, begin to cover; their stops are caught in many cases. Bulls who have been holding back come in and buy. The bull procession widens and deepens — more buyers, a greater number of stocks dealt in, a larger volume of trading all through the list.

And so the C. O. continues his operations on the bull side — with the characteristics of the market in its various phases much like one another in principle but differing in detail — until the bull wave has lasted so long and extended to so many stocks and brought in so many buyers that the C. O. is able not only to unload every last share of his long stocks; but, as his unloading such a large supply overcomes the remaining demand, he also begins to put out a line of shorts all through the list. He keeps on selling until all of the demand at the high level is satisfied. The market is now saturated with stocks and there is no buying power to lift that tremendous load which would have to be moved in order to advance prices to a new high level.

The C. O. sees this situation and knows that the time is ripe for a break. He bids up several leading high-priced stocks to new high levels, which causes the public to say: The averages are up into a new high. We should buy more.

Meanwhile he has been selling so many other stocks that their prices are sagging under the weight. He keeps on selling, getting out of the ones he bid up, and getting short of them also. Now he is adding every hour to the supply of stocks. The reaction has brought the public through the successive stages of hesitation to caution and then into a state of fear. That is, they fear the market is going down but they hope it will recover enough to let them out. This emotional conflict on the part of the public causes people to hang on and do nothing.

The market goes lower and lower because there are few buyers except occasional shorts covering. Prices are falling of their own weight. Supply is vastly heavier than demand. The C. O. has only to wait to realize a big profit on his shorts, to be added to the great profit he has already gathered on his longs. And with this vast sum at his command he knows that he can buy a tremendous number of stocks at the bottom of the decline, paying greatly reduced prices compared with those at which he sold.

Now I have explained all this so that you will get a clear idea of what is going on under the surface in the stock market. There is no Composite Operator, but the effect of the combined operations of bankers, pools, large operators, floor traders and the public is, when boiled down on the tape, of the same effect as if it were produced by one man's operations.

It is important that you observe the market from this standpoint, and that your trading operations be based, not on what you formerly regarded as the market's characteristics but on the fundamental law of supply and demand, which is at the bottom of every move that is made in every stock in the market at all times. It does not matter whether the buying and the selling, or both, are genuine or artificial: that is, manipulative — designed for a purpose: this law is working and will continue to work always.

The Old Timer was telling him about a ten-share trader who went long of Auburn in June, around 38, and made a 38-point profit in four days — in a bear market, mind you.

"Yes, I recall that move," he remarked sadly, "I was short. It cost me $42,000!"

"Just the difference between knowing how and guessing," said the Old Timer.

Wall Street Fallacies

2. That Success Depends on Having Enough Capital

" I 'VE been studying the stock market for a long time," remarked the young man, "and as soon as I get one or two thousand dollars capital I'll make a lot of money."

"You have the wrong idea," replied the Old Timer; "it is not capital you need, but knowledge. I'm willing to bucket all your trades — just between ourselves — up to the time you drop your two thousand, if you'll pay me as you lose. Millions of people just like you thought, up to 1929, that money was the first requisite; the past three years have demonstrated that regardless of how much capital a man has, if he doesn't know how, he'll lose most or all of it. I'll just give you a few examples:

"Hetty Green's son, Col. Green, told a friend of mine that at the top of the boom he had five hundred million dollars. By December, 1931, he said, this had shrunk to one hundred and twenty-five million. And I presume the following six months to the July '32 lows left him maybe less than a paltry hundred. Plenty of capital didn't help him any.

"Percy Rockefeller testified at the Washington hearing that he had lost many, many millions. John D's fortune is reputed to have shrunk to a fraction of its former size. Partners in big banking houses lost scores of millions. Pools composed of insiders did the same. The so-called 'Big Ten' were hopelessly sunk on the way down after making vast fortunes on the way up. As for the Investment Trusts," continued the Old Timer, "they lost billions of the public's money on your same mistaken idea — that money breeds success in the stock market.

"Now contrast the position of Andrew Mellon — in my opinion — the longest headed, farthest sighted financier in America. When the market was around the lows he wasn't broke; he was buying control of Bethlehem Steel in the open market. He had the money *because* he unloaded a lot of securities in the boom; money *grew out* of his knowledge.

"Have I proved that not money but *knowing how* is the biggest factor in the success of a trader or an investor?"

"But men like the Rockefellers and the big bankers are supposed to know all there is about the market. That's how they made their money, isn't it?" queried the young man.

"How much time do you suppose John D. and his son, or Percy R., spend studying the market?" asked Old Timer. "Very little; believe me, they're too much involved in their other large affairs. And so are the big bankers. As for the Investment Trusts, well there's no excuse for them at all. Only one that I recall (run by a man who has since died) took the short side and made a lot of money. That man knew the game — he was one in a million. Take my word for it, a lot of money is a big handicap to a chap who wants to learn how to trade in stocks successfully. If your judgment, young man, were one hundred per cent good you could build up a fortune starting with one hundred dollars; for you'd never take a loss. But as you can't be right all the time, you must suffer some losses.

"My advice to you," continued the Old Timer, "is this: When you think you can beat that old market, take a hundred dollars and prove it. If you succeed with that hundred you'll be a rare bird. If you lose it, dig up another and keep on that way till you get a hundred that will stick. Build on that one. Don't kid yourself that you need $1,000 or $2,000; that's too much like the rest of the public. Whenever you get a setback, find out why. Trade on both sides of the market. Ride 'em up and ride 'em down. Cut your losses and your profits will eventually outstrip them. Always present a thin edge to the enemy; never let him give you a broadside. But the main thing is: Keep at it till you really learn how, and then you won't need to worry where your capital is coming from."

Exploding the Dow Theory

THE test of any stock market theory is: How much money has it made for its most consistent followers? Many people are following this theory; some understand it, some do not. Mostly they are enthusiastic over it without exactly knowing why. So far we have never heard of a single trader or investor who has become hopelessly rich following it. If you know of any, tell us about them.

Now comes Alfred Cowles 3rd, of Colorado Springs, with a very interesting array of facts about the application of the theory by Dow and Hamilton — the latter being author of "The Stock Market Barometer" (1922). To quote from Mr. Cowles:

"The obvious source materials for such a study are Dow's editorials, Hamilton's editorials, and Hamilton's book. The vagueness of Dow's conclusions, and the brevity of his record, make analysis of his results impossible. Hamilton's book presents no complete current account of his applications of the theory. His editorials, however, are adequate in number, 255 in all, they extend over a 26 year period, and are sufficiently definite to allow scoring as bullish, bearish, or doubtful. These materials were derived from the files of the Wall Street Journal by Dr. Henry B. Kline of the University of Tennessee, in compliance with a request from a Dow Theory advocate, to assemble all editorials that dealt with stock market action. Dr. Kline was selected as a highly intelligent man who knew nothing of Hamilton, speculation, or the Dow Jones averages, to avoid any possible bias in selection. Editorials from 1903 to 1929 are ascribed to W. P. Hamilton because of his tacit claim to their authorship.

"Each of Hamilton's 255 editorials has been scored by majority vote of five readers as bullish, bearish, or doubtful. When doubtful it is assumed that he abstained from trading. When bullish it is assumed that he bought equal dollar amounts of the stocks in the Dow Jones railroad and industrial groups, and sold them only when he became bearish or doubtful. When bearish it is assumed that he sold short equal dollar amounts of these stocks, and covered only when he became doubtful or bullish. The percentage gain or loss on each such transaction is calculated, and the results accumulated through the 26 years. Since the Dow Jones averages have only recently been corrected for the effect of stock rights, stock dividends, and stock splits, it has been necessary to effect such adjustments through all the previous years. After this, the final step is to correct for the effect of brokerage charges, cash dividends, and the interest presumably earned by Hamilton when his funds were not in the market. The fully adjusted figures resulting are then reduced to an average annual figure which is the measure of the efficiency of the Dow method.

"Our final conclusion is that, from December 1903 to December 1929, the Dow method as interpreted by Hamilton earned a total return of exactly 12 per cent per annum compounded. In the same period the industrial group made a profit of 15.5 per cent per annum compounded. Hamilton therefore failed by a considerable margin to earn as much by his forecaster as he would have made by an outright continuous investment in the industrial averages. He exceeded by a wide margin, however, any normal investment return of about 6 per cent.

"Hamilton announced buy signals 27 times. In the industrial group 16 of these were profitable, 11 unprofitable. He gave sell signals 21 times, 10 were profitable, 11 unprofitable. He gave signals for retirement from the market 38 times, gaining money on 16, losing money on 22. In all, 44 of his forecasts were unsuccessful, 42 successful. The application of this test to the railroad group verifies these conclusions except that of the buying signals 14 were correct, 13 incorrect. Though the majority of Hamilton's short positions were unsuccessful, he made a slight addition to his principal through these operations, but less than average money rates. Hamilton undoubtedly rescued himself hurriedly from unfavorable positions, while he tended to let his profitable ones run. In the approximately horizontal industrial market from 1909 to 1914 inclusive, Hamilton's funds shrank 7.8 per cent per annum below what they would have been if put out at 5 per cent interest. In what proved ultimately to be an approximately horizontal market for two decades, Hamilton's record in the railroad group deserves notice. Through this almost horizontal secular market, Hamilton made an average annual gain of 5.7 per cent in rail stocks, equivalent to rather more than the return from money on call."

* * *

We have asked Mr. Cowles just what he meant by 12 per cent compounded; he replied, "I regret that I cannot supply you with the data showing what the profit or loss would have been by years, since the computation was not made on that basis. The profit or loss was computed for the periods determined by changes in Hamilton's forecasts and these, as you will readily understand, would not coincide with the termination of calendar years. The total profit which would have been made in the 26 years, by applying Hamilton's forecasts to the stocks composing the Dow Jones industrial averages, was 1804.95 per cent. This includes dividend and interest income, as well as adjustments for brokerage charges, stock dividends, rights, etc. Reducing this to an effective annual rate gives the profit of 12 per cent per annum, compounded annually, which was quoted in my letter."

Dividing the 26 years into 1,805 points, we get an average net return for the period of 7 per cent per annum. For each $1,000 of capital employed, there would be an average of less than $70 per year as profits on the predictions of Hamilton. This compounded would average $120 a year for the period.

Assuming one has the ability to interpret the Dow Theory as accurately as its chief interpreter, he would be taking a highly speculative position in the market for a

possible one or two per cent over what he would gain per
annum if he invested his money in sound bonds. But there
is no assurance that anyone can do this. Nothing that has
occurred in the past is any indication of what can be accomplished by this means in the future. The average trader
could probably not have done so well.

Operating on the Dow Theory involves a series of unlimited risks. Conditions in the market are constantly
changing and there is no assurance that a follower of this
theory can average even three per cent per annum in profits
for the next 26 years.

The greatest danger arises from the fact that so many
people are now following the Dow Jones Averages (or think
they are) that it is an easy matter for manipulators to juggle
the stocks of which these averages are composed, so as to
make its followers buy and sell when the manipulators so
desire.

Our observation of it is this: The so-called Dow method
is as modern as an ice-wagon, and just as cumbersome. It is
as clear as mud. Much of the time it gets you in or out miles
from the real turning points in the market. It is of no use in
actual trading compared with modern ways of judging the
market known to many people. As Hamilton himself wrote
about that pet part of the theory in which one average
breaks out of a line, this indication is "sometimes misleading," "frequently misleading," "constantly misleading,"
"independent and therefore untrustworthy," "usually
deceptive or invariably deceptive." All these terms Hamilton
employed in describing the break-through feature of one
average. As to the "confirmation" given by one average to
the other, he uses among others, the terms, "more apt to be
deceptive than not." And "merely a coincidence when it
happens to occur."

People who for the first time become attracted to the
Dow theory have been known to grin like a boy who has
picked up a horseshoe; but the longer they study it, the less
they are inclined to grin.

The Real Value in the Financial Page of Your Newspaper

EVERY day twenty million people read forty million financial pages in their newspapers. Average reading time fifteen minutes per paper — half an hour per person per day; ten million hours a day devoted to the reading of financial news. What do the readers get in return?

How much time do *you* devote to the financial page? Just what do *you*, Mr. Average Man, get out of it? You reply: "I read my financial page at the breakfast table or on my way to and from the office, and it keeps me posted. I know what is going on in Wall Street. It enables me to watch my stocks and to become aware of anything that is likely to affect the market or my holdings." Actually you are not thus able to watch your stocks; you merely read what *has happened* to them. As for "becoming aware," a thousand things can affect them before you know it.

Can you trace actual profits to this "keeping posted and watching your holdings"? Profits, I believe, arise from the purchase of stocks at lower prices than those at which they are sold. Does your newspaper actually aid you in this?

The vital quality in speculation is foresight. Does your newspaper help you to cultivate foresight—to anticipate coming events? If you have any foresight, was it generated from your perusal of the financial page?

Average Man's summary, if he be fair with himself, would be something like this: "I cannot cultivate foresight from my newspapers' financial pages, but at least I can learn how the market in general, and my stocks in particular, have been performing. I never buy or sell because of what I read in the text; my judgment is influenced more by the tips and the advice of my broker, his customers' man, and my friends. I am willing to admit that I get some real dope from one of the clerks in a leading bank; he has made me more money than all the newspapers I ever read."

I do not claim it to be the function of a financial editor to turn out a column that can be converted into profits by traders and investors. Rarely are newspapers in the advisory business, although some have at times had the temerity to venture into this difficult and precarious field. At least one newspaper that I know of contains actual trading advice; on this you can take chances — if you think it likely that you can make a profit on advice which costs two cents.

And then the Brokers' Opinions: Over any given period and without reflection on any one in particular, these, as a whole, are correct about half the time. Some firms average better than others. Usually the firms publishing their opinions are equally divided between the bull and bear side of the market. Most people find this rather confusing.

There are many other features of the average financial page: Hints to Investors, Corporation Reports, Trade News, Money Market, Stock Averages, Commodity Prices, The Curb, Bond Transactions; various articles, comments and market reports. But how can any one take the day's gathering of these and interpret the mass into: What to do — buy, sell, hold or stay neutral? *No one* can do this with profit in the long run.

* * *

What am I getting at? Next to the tape of the stock ticker in its market importance, the financial page of your newspaper contains a most valuable aid to profit-making in the table recording the day's transactions in stocks — the opening, highest, lowest and closing prices; the number of shares bought and sold. That table contains real information; *reliable* information; *inside* information. It records both history and prophecy. When you know how to analyze it, you will quickly discard all the other text, tables and whatnot, for it will tell you the only thing worth knowing about the stock market — what is *likely* to happen.

The table will also inform you which stocks are the most desirable to buy, sell, hold or which to avoid; and this with a far higher percentage of accuracy than if you depend on the news, reviews, gossip, reports or opinions.

No broker or customers' man, banker or investors' counsel, can do as much for you as you can accomplish for yourself by extracting all there is to be found in the record of the transactions. Between the lines and the columns there flows evidence of the Law of Supply and Demand — the dominating factor in the stock market — that always tells the truth; that never fails; that never changes.

If we would take money out of Wall Street, we should understand the operation of that Law. This accomplished, there may be certain phases of the market that may puzzle us, but for only brief periods. And so in reading the financial page, enlightened operators in stocks will discard the news and the opinions and the other features; but they will the more highly value their newspapers when they realize all the stock table means to them in profit possibilities.

To read the financial page only for the purpose of "keeping posted and seeing how one's stocks stand" is to take a gun and go hunting for flies where deer and pheasants abound.

*Nightmare of a trader who failed
to use stop orders*

More Inside Information

A SUBSCRIBER writes: Not long ago, my broker inquired by phone if I had "noticed the behavior of Westinghouse lately." With considerable enthusiasm he urged the purchase of the stock. I asked his reasons. He said, "I know the crowd that operates in this issue; I feel that I understand the stock thoroughly and it is my observation that a move in this issue usually starts on a Thursday. I have the inside report that it will be manipulated ten points higher within the coming week. You better get on it at once and participate in this move."

If I had been susceptible to this sort of urgent advice I would have immediately purchased the stock without further investigation. I realized, however, that the wise thing to do was to review the behavior of this issue during the past several sessions. I found the stock already had recorded a considerable advance and that it had been meeting supply for several days past. In fact, it looked to me as though the move he predicted had already taken place and that a reversal of trend was imminent. I refused to grab the bait, but watched developments.

Within a day or two the stock advanced one or two points above the level at which it had been recommended. Thereafter, the supply apparently increased; the stock began to back away from supply around its top levels, met persistent offerings on the minor bulges from day to day and finally, with considerable increase in volume, broke sharply about ten points, thereby recording a movement almost exactly the opposite of the broker's prediction.

Not long after this, the volume of trading in Westinghouse began to dry up. Day after day its action became more sluggish; it seemed to refuse to go lower. This went on for about a week and the stock began to take on the appearance of absorption, if not actual accumulation for a substantial rally. Imagine my surprise therefore, when my broker friend again called me on the telephone and advised me that Westinghouse was acting badly, was about to break wide open, that "all the boys in the office" were selling it short; that holders were unloading as rapidly as they could without actually breaking the market and that the manipulators who were seldom wrong, were planning to let it settle down for about ten points.

I did not remind the broker of his previous recommendation, but again I refused to take the bait and decided once more to investigate the situation in considerable detail. It seemed to me that on its technical action the stock was an attractive purchase and that it could logically be bought with a stop of not over one or two points. Within a day or two the price began to rise, slowly at first, then on slightly increased volume. The minor reactions did not reach down to the previous lows. The volume persisted in drying up during the little downward movements from day to day. Eventually the activity broke out on the up side and the stock rallied vigorously — about eight points.

I did not call my friend's attention to results of his two forecasts, for I saw no reason to embarrass him. Furthermore, I felt that he might in the future give me advice of a similar nature which might call my attention to a circumstance that would justify the actual "coppering" of his advice in situations with which he claimed to be thoroughly familiar. I believe he was entirely conscientious as to what he believed to be two attractive opportunities for trading, but that he was himself misled by "inside" information.

———

It is a cardinal folly of human nature to believe what one wants to believe rather than what is so, and to love to hear what is pleasant rather than what is true.

Philosophy of Jay Gould

Second of a series containing extracts from the wisdom of famous Wall
Street operators*

A MAN who is liable to rapid thinking very often ar-
rives at conclusions without being able to tell the
process, and he is satisfied the conclusions are correct; and
yet if you undertake to give the evidence by which they are
reached, you could not tell how it was done.

* * *

Because I managed to get several million dollars in the
period that the ordinary man gets a few hundred is no
crime in itself. Besides it must be remembered that every
one of my transactions was essentially a gamble. They have
in the main, been successful, but my risk has always been
great. One misstep, one important failure, and I would have
gone the way of James Keene or Cyrus Field or Henry
Smith.

* * *

In Wall Street there are several types of men. There is
the man who is by nature a builder. He is only incidentally
in Wall Street because that is our financial center. His activities are mainly in enterprises scattered about the country, in all of which he is deeply interested. This type, the
builder or projector, is not always a good trader. He visions
enterprises and sees them through in the physical aspect. If
he starts a railroad he sees the road through from the very
beginning to the very end. His satisfaction comes from ac-
complishment. Vanderbilt was an example of a successful
projector.

The second type of man in Wall Street is the banker. He

* From "Jay Gould — The Story of a Fortune," by Robert Irving
Warshow. Greenberg, Publisher, Inc., New York.

acquires money by possession and its adroit use. Morgan was an example of a clever banker.

The third type, the real Wall Street man, the man whose interests are bounded by the East River and Trinity Church, is the speculator, the manipulator, the stock gambler, if you will. This type, the manipulator, must first be a good trader. The old clothes man is in a sense a good trader if he can persuade you to part with the suit you need, but his imagination is limited to your back doorstep. The small dealer is a trader. "It looks like snow, boys," said the Finns, for they had snowshoes to sell. They believed in advertising, and they worked by suggestion. That is why we use Ivory soap.

But the large manipulator, besides being by nature a trader, must have an active imagination which sees things in broad outlines. He must envision what is not visible, he must believe in this seeming mirage, and must have the courage and the nerve to gamble on the product of the imagination. The man who conceives complicated plans, sees them through clearly in his mind and has the courage of his faith, — that man may be a manipulator. These are some of his affirmative qualities; but there must also be lacking in him, at least until business is over, those lovable human frailties which go under the name of pity, of generosity, of mercy.

If the story of the men that Wall Street made rich were written, it would fill several books. If the story of the men that Wall Street made rich and then broke were written, it would fill a library. These men who became rich were in almost every case men of ability, good traders, and keen business men, but they overplayed their hand. They knew when to come in, but they didn't know when to get out. The perfect speculator, the perfect gambler, if you will, must know when to come in; more important, he must know when to stay out; and, most important, he must know when to get out once he is in.

Editorial

M ANY people ask me, What will put this market up? This is my answer:

Steady absorption of stocks has continued all through these years of depression. When prices were declining, the supply of stocks more than filled the demand; but since June 1932, demand has gradually overcome supply. It is an old Wall Street saying that the same stock can be liquidated but once.

Examine the total number of stockholders of corporations with shares listed on the N. Y. Stock Exchange and you will find a remarkable increase in the past few years. While many of our wealthiest men have been liquidating, the five-, ten- and twenty-share buyers have been picking up stocks, slowly but steadily.

Accumulation does not always mean that large interests have been buying, but that stocks are going out of weak hands into the strong boxes of those who buy outright. Many fortunes will be realized by those who have thus acquired what others were forced to sacrifice.

Sooner or later the effect of this buying will be felt. The public is not organized and cannot act in concert as the big operators do, but the continued absorption will become forcefully apparent when, acting upon some especially favorable developments, those who have postponed buying begin to take on substantial amounts.

Listed on the Stock Exchange are 1,300,000,000 shares of stocks. Every share is held by someone. An advance of one point in the average prices adds one and one-third billions of dollars to the equities of the owners. Ten points means thirteen billions!

That much increase in values will generate courage — the vital element now lacking. Instill courage into the hearts of stockholders and their timid, hidden money will begin to come out. It will be used to buy stocks, clothing, merchandise, automobiles, real estate and everything down the line. Business will begin to improve because of the release of that pent-up buying demand.

If I controlled vast capital and sufficient buying power, I would advance this market slowly but steadily. I would keep it going. Such a rise in the stock market would, of itself, produce an improvement in business. The multiple problems with which the public is now so deeply concerned — finance, taxation, bad business and unemployment — would fade into the background were there to be flashed across the country and around the world the electrifying, rallying cry: *The Stock Market is going up!*

My suggestion is that every person who is now a holder of any stock listed on the N. Y. Stock Exchange buy five additional shares, more or less, of the same or any other common stock, according to his or her resources.

If 20,000,000 stockholders thus buy an average of five shares each, their aggregate purchases would be 100,000,000 shares, or at the rate of 1,000,000 shares for the next 100 Stock Exchange sessions.

A made-to-order bull market should result.

The average prices of stocks should thus be advanced 50% over the prices ruling March 1st. This would mean a rise of some $25 a share in stocks selling from $50 to $100, and increase the equities of all stockholders by some thirty billions of dollars!

Here is an acorn from which a very tall oak can be made to grow.

Note: The above was written in February 1933.

Analysis of 4½ Years of Forecasting by 41 Advisory Services and Publications

IN THE beginning, I suppose, there were just brokers and clients. Stock market science did not exist. The clients had to do their own guessing, take tips, trade on their own or others' opinions.

Then someone hatched the idea of using charts. By this means they worked out mechanical systems. Look over the files of the New York *Herald* in the 90's and you will find the Sunday edition carrying two or three pages of ads from "market letter writers," who used charts. There were three entrances to one office with a different name on each door and respective subscription prices running $2, $5 and $10 per month. All three letters were written by the same man from the same set of charts.

Then there was an old boy whose ads were headed "Wagner Warns." His real name was Smith. He stuttered badly and no one seemed more amused at this than he. You had to stutter your way through his market letters; they were written that way. His fame began with a warning headed, "Beware the Ides of March," which preceded a big break in the market. Probably he is now warning St. Peter.

Along about 1908, there began to appear a more dignified type of advisers who called themselves investment experts. Certain ones had never spent a year in Wall Street in their whole lives, but they were willing to tell just how the trick should be turned. Some were worse than others. At times the best of them had a measure of success and worked up a big following; but it is a fluctuating business, and one good year is not necessarily followed by another.

Twenty years later: The profession began to take on a

new title — Investment Counsel. Much more dignified. Impressive. A counsel is supposed to know something the other fellow doesn't. But of course you have to take your chances. Now the woods are full of counsellors. A trip around the United States will disclose any number of them. Many give the impression of having lost all their money in the stock market; so they are now engaged in telling others how to beat the game. But there are a few good ones — don't misunderstand me.

No objection can be raised against anyone going into the business, provided he has been successful himself, either in trading or advising others. To be a good adviser does not mean that one must be a good trader: the two abilities do not always go together. The judgment of some deteriorates badly with their own money at stake; they are better able to advise when unbiassed by their own commitments. In some instances, however, certain individuals have continued in this business with a long record of failures. How they can have the nerve to go on year after year inviting subscriptions is a mystery to most. They get away with it because new players are constantly sitting in to replace those who have dropped out.

But if it is a legitimate business for those who can qualify, what has been the record of the years 1929–33? Has anyone made an outstanding success in this field? Perhaps I am not well posted but folks tell me practically all the prophets have fallen down one way or another. Some got them out at the top, but in again too soon. Others stayed bearish too long. How is one to know whom to follow?

It is an axiom in Wall Street that if a man seems to know ten percent more than his neighbor the latter will lean upon him. Livermore put it: "The average man desires to be told specifically which particular stock to buy or sell. He wants to get something for nothing. He does not wish to work. He doesn't even wish to have to think."

Whenever I notice a trader studying a market letter I recall seeing a mother chewing her baby's crackers. Those whose stock market crackers are masticated for them will never develop their own teeth. Venturing money on another's judgment of the stock market is merely betting that he will be right. Your own judgment is used only in deciding whether his tip may be better than some other. It is difficult to see how a man can become an expert in deciding the comparative money-making value of tips.

Some advisory concerns have developed large organizations, under the delusion that better judgment can be derived from a company of men than from an individual; but I have not observed that accuracy of advices improves in proportion to the increase in the number of associates or employees. Quite the contrary: *The undiluted judgment of one man who really knows is usually far better than any mixture of opinions.*

About five years ago Mr. Alfred Cowles 3rd, of Colorado Springs, determined to analyze the forecasting ability of sixteen advisory services and twenty-five financial publications. His purpose was to prove the quality of their work in (1) predicting future movements of the stock market or (2) in selecting common stocks which should prove superior in investment merit to the general run of equities.

"The forecasters included well-known organizations in the different fields represented," said Mr. Cowles in presenting this paper before a meeting of the American Statistical Association in Cincinnati December 31, 1932. "Many of these are large and well financed, employing economists and statisticians of unquestioned ability. Some of the forecasters seem to have taken a page from the book of the Delphic Oracle, expressing their prophesies in terms susceptible of more than one construction. It would frequently be possible, therefore, for an editor, after the event, to present a plausible challenge of our interpretation." For this reason and "since their publication would be likely to invite wholesale controversies over the interpretation of their records, the names of these organizations have been omitted."

According to this analysis, the work of sixteen leading financial services was examined over the four and a half years ending July, 1932. These services made a practice of regularly submitting to their subscribers selected lists of common stocks for investment. About 7500 separate recommendations were made and the analysis required approximately 75,000 entries. The most unbiassed attitude was maintained in order to secure an accurate conclusion. Results were tabulated every six months. The percentage gain or loss on each transaction was recorded, and in a parallel column the gain or loss in the stock market averages. Thus a fair comparison was made.

Only six of the sixteen services showed any profit at all. These ranged from six to twenty per cent. Spread over a period of four and a half years this would mean an average of from 1 plus per cent to 4 plus per cent per annum. The other ten services showed from no profit to a 33% loss. The average annual effective rate of all the services, according to Mr. Cowles, was a loss of 1.43%. That is just a little less than no profit at all for a person who subscribed to and followed all the services.

Mr. Cowles also analyzed results secured in forecasting the course of the stock market by 24 financial publications, among which were 18 professional financial services, 4 financial weeklies, 1 bank letter and 1 investment house letter. In all, 4,000 forecasts were tabulated for the period from January 1, 1928, to June 1, 1932. Only one of the 24 forecasters recommended short commitments. (Note that a bear market prevailed for nearly three years of the period mentioned.)

RESULTS OF FORECASTS BY 24 FINANCIAL PUBLICATIONS

Forecaster	Period	
1	104 weeks	+ 72.4 per cent
2	230	+ 31.5
3	230	+ 28.3
4	22	+ 24.2
5	156	+ 9.0
6	52	+ 3.0
7	91	+ 2.4
8	52	+ 1.3
9	104	− 1.7
10	156	− 2.1
11	230	− 3.6
12	43	− 6.0
13	52	− 6.7
14	130	− 6.9
15	230	−12.5
16	52	−13.5
17	230	−17.2
18	69	−21.5
19	230	−29.4
20	230	−33.0
21	230	−35.3
22	230	−41.5
23	156	−45.3
24	230	−49.1

As Mr. Cowles has stated, "The records show that only one-third of the list met with any success." After proper weighting and adjustments, he concluded "that the averaged forecasting agency fell approximately 4% per annum below a record representing the average of all performances achievable by pure chance. This would seem to indicate that in general these stock market forecasters failed to accomplish their objective."

Mr. Cowles further explained: "The most that can be said in extenuation is that the long, continued decline in securities has been, naturally, a handicap to a group which, taking warning from the experience of Cassandra, usually seems constrained to look on the bright side. During the four and a half year period under analysis the number of weeks in which the stock market declined almost exactly equalled the number of weeks in which advances were recorded, and the total amount of the declines considerably exceeded the total amount of the advances. Yet we recorded during this period 2,221 bullish forecasts as against 810 bearish forecasts and 544 doubtful. As further evidence of failure on the part of the forecasters, it is worthy of note that 1928, the only year in which the market registered more gains than losses, was the only year in which the number of bullish forecasts did not exceed the bearish by a wide margin."

By an ingenious method of using cards, numbered, shuffled and drawn, a comparison was made of the results above recorded with those which would have been obtained by depending upon pure chance. In order to compare these chance predictions with those made by the twenty-four professional agencies, the following chart has been prepared showing all the records, actual and hypothetical. This chart indicates that even the greatest gains made by the forecasters were equalled by the best of the twenty-four

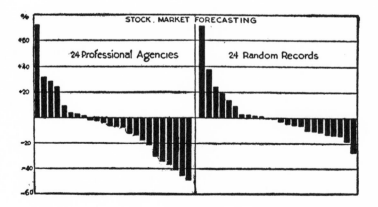

imaginary actions representing random actions at random intervals. But the losses made by the forecasters were much greater than those registered by the least successful of the twenty-four records of pure chance operations.

If you wish to take chances with any advisory service, why not do it with limited risk? You might reason thus: It costs, say $100 a year, to learn whether this service will yield a profit or not. If its advices are unprofitable and I follow them with cash, I must add to the $100 subscription price my total losses, and compare these with my profits; the difference will indicate the price I paid for the year's service. But if I merely make a record of their advices and follow them "on paper" for a year, this will give me a line on the quality of judgment I am buying as a substitute for my own. My risk will thus be limited to the $100 paid for the subscription. The publishers, of course, do not insist that I trade on their advices with real money.

It is not my job to act as a Wall Street censor, particularly among those who are engaged in advisory work. In that field I have many friends. No one understands their difficulties better, for I spent fifteen years in advisory work up to 1926, and have had my share of both knocks and boosts. But, in the light of Mr. Cowles' unbiassed analysis, it would seem that the profession needs reorganizing — ED.

* * *

Trading without scientifically limiting your risk is like wearing your pants without a belt or suspenders.

Run Your Own Pool

WHY join pools? Flocking together carries no assurance of profit, for your success depends on who is running the pool and how good a trader he is — how far-sighted, how expert, how clever.

Plenty of pools go wrong. Remember the testimony before the 1932 Congressional Investigating Committee. The biggest of them fall down when they buck the trend or misjudge the market.

Joining a pool is merely a confession that some other fellow who is put in command of the outfit knows more about the market than you do. Or that particular stock. You are just taking chances on his judgment.

Your Pool Manager was once totally ignorant of the market; now you are paying him a percentage to run a pool in which you are interested. Perhaps to a degree, he has mastered the art of trading in stocks and can do it more successfully than you can.

* * *

Your Pool Manager has a different way of operating from that of the outsider. His purpose is identical — to make a profit, but he has a different slant on the problem.

He is continually trying to mark down his cost. His original line is accumulated at a low level. He sells some on the bulges and takes this back on the dips. These profits reduce the cost of his original line. He makes the bulges in order to bring in outside buying and to enable him to sell.

Always he keeps an account of how much he is long and his average price — that is his position. He must continually foresee coming changes in the market and adjust his position accordingly. If he sees danger to his long position, he will get out and go short. He does not concern himself so much with the direction of the trend as he does with his ability to detect what is likely to happen, so that he will be on the right side when it does happen.

The individual trader who operates his own account can follow the same tactics, except that he cannot produce the bulges. Suppose he trades in fifty, one hundred or five hundred share lots: he gets long at the bottom of the swing, anticipating a twenty point rise with frequent strong spots and reactions. He can always divide his line into four or five lots, even though he be an odd lot trader, and he can sell part of his line on manipulative bulges made for the purpose of letting the insider out of part of his line. Then he can take back this lot on a dip and thus mark down his average cost. Just because you have a few hundred shares of stock, there is no reason why you should sit still with it in your lap waiting for some beautiful thing to happen to it.

After you have sold part of your holdings, the market goes on up: well, you have some more to sell and there is no reason to complain. Or if your stock is declining you can buy back what you have already sold, providing indications are favorable.

What we are trying to emphasize is the advantage of maintaining a fluid, flexible position instead of a rigid one; this calls for a mind that acts like quicksilver instead of maintaining a rigidity like steel.

A more professional attitude toward the market will enhance your net profit at the end of the year. Every man is either progressing or deteriorating as to his trading ability. It is well to develop improved expertness instead of merely following the time-worn and loss-producing mental attitude that most of the public hold toward the market.

———

I like Wall Street because you stand a chance of making money there so much faster than you can in the slow-poke ways of regular business. One turn of two or three points in shares will, if you are on the right side and have put out a big enough line, net you as much money in six days as an ordinary business would in six months.—DANIEL DREW.

Annuities — 100% Security

ONLY one class of people came through the panic without shrinkage in their principal or their income: I refer to those who depended upon annuities. All other classes of securities, real estate and every kind of property shrunk in value from 1929 to '33, and as someone owned every share of stock, every bond and every piece of other property, practically everyone suffered to a greater or lesser degree. But those whom the insurance companies agreed to pay an income for life or for a certain period of years came through practically undamaged.

One case, especially, impressed me, that of an elderly woman. Starting with about $10,000 she had accumulated about $25,000 profit in the bull market up to 1928. She expressed the desire to secure herself against loss and poverty in her old age. I found that she had no relatives and therefore she was justified in putting all her money into annuities. Selecting several of the strongest companies, I had her funds distributed at the rate of $4,000 in each. As her age was then 68, she was able to secure something over $300 a month for life.

From that day to this, she has had no financial worries of any kind. Her income checks have come along with cease-less regularity. They are spread through the twelve months so as roughly to equalize the periods of payment. She has travelled merrily about Europe and America with no con-cern whatever as to the condition of the stock market, financial institutions or business.

Here is an example for all of us, especially those who make big money in bull markets and are mostly washed out by the out-going tide. How often do we consummate a successful campaign in the stock market, then take the money out and soak it away in what we call investment securities? But a safe deposit box is no guarantee against shrinkage and so during this liquidation and depression we found our backlogs shrunken to about the size of chips. Not so with our insurance policies or (if any) our annuities; for while the insurance companies have also suffered losses during the panic, with one or two exceptions (small and temporary) all have come through, paid their annuity checks, death claims and made their loans without compromise or curtailment. No other kind of investment has maintained such a high percentage of face value — not even U. S. Government Bonds.

George S. Van Schaick, Superintendent of Insurance of the State of New York, has stated: *No policyholder in legal reserve life insurance companies licensed to do business in the State of New York has suffered one dollar of loss, either in loan value or otherwise.*

There is a lesson in this for everyone; for who anticipated the devastating results of the panic and its aftermath? Very few made any provision for it. Everything we had were properties that shrunk in value. Only our insurance investments proved to be panic-proof.

Think of the millions of dollars that could have been taken out of the stock market while prices were high and put where they would have yielded a sure monthly or quarterly return, enabling their owners to carry themselves and their families through the panic, avoiding untold losses, sacrifices, bankruptcies and suicides.

Let us therefore resolve, that in the next boom we will know better than to have all of our worldly goods in things that shrink, and that we shall, when the next panic comes around, have at least a part of our profits where they will be safe from the bears. Let us buy *Income* — not "Insecurities."

Note: Those interested in this suggestion will find an exceptionally satisfactory article entitled, "One Way to Security in Old Age," by G. W. Fitch on page 395 of the December, 1932, *American Mercury.* Also a boil-down of that article in the *Reader's Digest* for January, 1933.

Spotting the Turning Points

THIS is one of the most difficult feats in judging the stock market. Very few traders or investors can do this. It requires expert knowledge and long experience.

There are several different kinds of turning points: that of the day's swing — the high or low spot for a single session; or the end of a 3 to 5 point swing; or of a 10 to 30 point swing. But most important of all, and the most difficult, is spotting the *final* culminating point: where a bull market finally ends and a bear market begins.

And there *is* a top day — for the whole market (based on the averages) and for every single stock. It is, of course, not the same day for every issue; some begin to slide off weeks and months before others; but the records show when the final high wave breaks; that is the psychological moment for getting out of everything.

How many were able to see and to act correctly on the

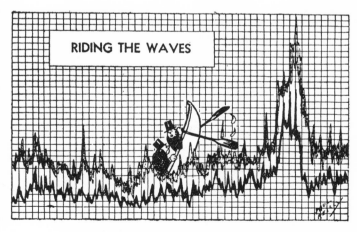

"Ye Gods, Ed! We'll never make it!"

— *Ballyhoo*

final turning point when the bull market ended in early September, 1929? Very few.

If you are in the market you should begin at once to cultivate the knowledge that will enable you, next time, to do this vital thing — spot the top. You may argue that tops like 1929 don't occur often enough for us to recognize them. That is both true and untrue. If we study the characteristics — the symptoms — that occur on the tops of the small swings (the daily, the 3 to 5 point and the 10 to 30 point) we find that they display indications that are similar to those of the big tops, just as a drop of sea water analyzes the same as a bucketful.

But if we ignore these facts; if we fail to learn; then we must naturally expect to find ourselves again loaded with long stocks at high prices when the top of the next bull market is recorded.

Blaming our broker or some one else will not then get our money back; we shall have no one to blame but ourselves. Not only can one learn to observe and to act on the turning points; he can go farther and become aware of their *approach*. By thus anticipating them, he can unload as close to the apex as any one can reasonably expect.

And when you have done this rare and desirable thing, the money you will thus release for buying when the *bear* market ends will pay for several times as many shares at bargain prices.

_____

MORE INSIDE INFORMATION

A trader writes: I personally know a man who has been associated with one of our largest corporations for nearly thirty years. He holds a responsible position with that company, and knows more about its inner workings than any average outsider. Early in July, last year, based upon what he knew about the company's immediately past and future prospects, he sold his last 500 shares at 24 with the expectation of re-purchasing it at 15. At the very moment he was selling out, your way of forecasting indicated it was going from 24 to 40. It more than made good by rising above 42, which again proves that the action of the market is a safer guide than the opinion of any insider.

Maxims of Daniel Drew*

Third of a series of extracts from the writings and sayings of famous Wall Street operators

I BECAME an operator in the New York Stock Exchange; I hung out my shingle on Broad Street. . . . If a fellow can make money selling a critter just after she has drunk up fifty pounds of water, what can't he make by issuing a lot of new shares of a railroad or steamboat company, and then selling this just as though it was the original shares?

* * *

I was a middle-aged man on the Street when Jim Fisk was a baby in the cradle, and before Jay Gould had seen the light of day. I might almost say I was their Wall Street parent. Many of their schemes and methods they learned from me. I was the pioneer. The way to manipulate stocks and work Wall Street dickers was well-nigh unknown when I first went into the business. I thought up many of the schemes out of my own brain. Those who came after had nothing to do but copy my ideas. Gould and Fisk — they were pupils of mine, both of them. I helped to make them. They were a pair of colts; I broke them in. It is easy now to lay out a campaign for working the market. But back in my early days, it wasn't so easy by a long shot. I had to invent ways of doing it. I had no guides to steer by.

* * *

It is always an advantage in Wall Street operations to be on the inside of a railroad or a big industrial concern. You know, then, the monthly earnings before they are given out to the public. You get earliest notice of any favorable or unfavorable happening. You have access to the transfer books and know where all the circulating stock is. Any dangers that have arisen to the road's property, or any new connection favorable to the road's earning capacity, is

*From THE BOOK OF DANIEL DREW, by Bouck White. Copyright 1910 by Doubleday, Doran & Co., Inc.

known to you long before the outside investors have got the tip. So that you can go onto the Stock Exchange and speckilate in those shares with your eyes open, whilst the rest of the speckilators are going it blind. An insider's position is as good as money in the chest.

Besides, I had now another advantage as well. Not only could I predict well-nigh every turn in Erie shares. I could do even better. I could make it turn in either direction I chose. I had the horse by the halter, so to speak, and could lead him where I wanted. If my operations on the Stock Exchange made it needful for the stock to go up, I could give out that the road was prosperous — and her stock would go up. Or if I was in a bearish temper and wanted her shares to slump, I could make the road unprosperous for a time, and then stocks would go down to the point where I wanted them.

I had found ways of using its shares in Wall Street whereby I could sometimes make a turn of ten points in Erie inside of a month. A stock that bobs back and forth as suddenly as that, is going to be followed by a great crowd of speckilators.

What's the use of being on the inside if you don't have the advantage over speckilators who are on the outside?

* * *

In order to start a bear campaign, you must first balloon the stock sky-high. Because when you are a bear you sell when the stock is high, and deliver when the stock is low (that is, if the deal turns out right). Your profit is the difference between those two figures — the greater the difference, the greater your profit. Besides, it is usually easier to put out a line of shorts when the market is high. Through some kink or other in human nature, the ordinary run of people are bullish and hopeful towards a stock when it's high. The stock has gone up so finely, they suppose it's going to keep on going up, and you usually find them ready buyers of your short sales.

Figure Charts

ALL forms of charts record market history. Some give this in great detail; others like Figure Charts are not so exact, but they have their advantages.

Just as you measure anything in inches, feet, or miles without recording the fractions, so Figure Charts take into consideration the moves from one full figure to another. Figure Charts discard all fractions: also the factors time and volume.

If we were floor traders, operating for small fractions, everything must be calculated. Or, if we are trading from the tape and getting in and out the same day, then every fraction, every fluctuation of one-eighth or more and every transaction, carrying its weight of evidence, becomes important. But if we are interested in getting in right on the main swings of the market, say from ten to thirty points, we can discard the fractions and get a better result.

Practically all units of measurement are used in various ways: to record, to estimate, to study and to forecast. Just so with Figure Charts. The one-point Figure Chart is the standard for stocks that are neither very high nor very low. When we get down into the single figures a different form of Figure Chart is advisable and still another when we get up into the two hundreds and three hundreds.

The value of any chart depends upon the ability of the operator to interpret it so that he may, by its aid, refresh his memory; make his forecasts; extract profits from the market. No chart is of any use whatever unless it can be interpreted with accuracy. A chart is a transposed tape; it is merely a tool which aids a stock trader. He records on his chart what *has* happened; then estimates what is *likely* to happen. The more he studies it the more benefit he derives — from the Figure Chart or any other form of chart.

Can you read this chart?

It shows all the one point movements of Atchison around 18 — its low point in July 1932, where it turned upward for a rise to 64.

To 64 ↑

```
31                                                           31
30                                                           30
29        29  29  29                              28  28     29
30        28  28                                  27  27     28  28
28                                                26         27  27
          26                          25          25
          25                          24  24  24
          24                    23  23  23  23
          23                    22  22  22
          22              23 23 21
          21              22 22 20
                    22    21
                    21    20
              21 21 20
              20 20 19
              19 19
                 18
```

The action of Atchison at that time gave *ten distinct buy signals* from 18 to 24. It kept *urging* you to buy.

If you *know* these signals you have an understanding of Stock Market Technique. If not you can learn them.

Such a chart gives you *better* and *more re-* *liable information* than any insider or other adviser can give you. Its forecasts and predictions work out to a high percentage of accuracy.

If you had bought 100 shares of Atchison when this chart told you to buy, around 20, you could have sold it at 60 within six weeks — a profit of $4,000.

Don't Overvalue the News

FOR some days before the French Government announced its decision people were telling me that if
France did not pay things would "go to the dogs." Wall
Street seemed to have its mind centered on this $20,000,-
000 item to the exclusion of all other considerations.

The action of the market kept saying: Stocks are being
bought on the decline. The demand is better than the
supply. Confidence seems to be returning. There are more
buyers than sellers. We don't really care whether France
pays or not. $20,000,000 is small change.

The tape was contradicting the popular impression.
The market had weighed this item and found little or nothing bearish about it; so when the news came out, prices
merely backed off a fraction and waited for the sellers to
get through. Leading stocks like Telephone, Can, Union
Pacific, Steel and United Aircraft went off on an average of
less than a point; then the market turned dead. What
better evidence could anyone ask of the monetary trend?
What better proof that they were wrong who predicted
disaster would follow default?

If you must read the news, do not try to convert it into
stock market profits, for you will fail except on rare occa-
sions. In the net, you will lose money.

Stock Market Prices Fluid

Stock market prices are, in one sense, fluid, inasmuch as
they invariably follow the line of least resistance. No one
can tell how long or how far this line will lead in a certain
direction, but the evidence that it will change, or has
changed, is clearly apparent to one who is experienced in
judging the market by its own action; although interrup-
tions and reversals, due to unexpected causes, frequently
compel swift alterations of opinion.

THE purpose of this publication is to be helpful to the public that brings its money to Wall Street for various reasons, mostly speculative.

We endeavor to demonstrate that speculation without knowledge is dangerous — often disastrous, and that depending on the advice of others is also hazardous.

We maintain that unless one learns how to trade intelligently and scientifically he should avoid the stock market and attend to the business or the profession he understands.

We claim that stock trading is an art or a science; that it can be learned and successfully followed as an avocation or as a profession.

We do not sell or give advice on the market or on securities.

We have no affiliations with any other publishing concern.

Flashes

Hearsay is half lies.

Cheap advice is plentiful.

All that is in peril is not lost.

Never buy an egg until it is laid.

Where certainty ends speculation begins.

A profit is not a profit until it is realized.

It is better to lose the saddle than the horse.

Take advice only from those who have been successful.

Inside information has wrecked many a big bank account.

Do not expect your ship to come in unless you have sent one out.

The underlying principles of all market movements are practically the same.

Money is made by anticipating when a stock is going to move from one trading area to another.

As a means of money-making, trading in stocks is *potentially* the most profitable of all pursuits.

Do you want to know why most people lose money in stocks? Listen to the chatter in any broker's office.

The public is apt to follow the vague and the glittering rather than the substantial and the detailed.

A few fat years are no indication that you can trade successfully. The test is: Are the lean years getting less lean?

What this country needs most is *not* a good five-cent cigar, but a thorough understanding of the stock market.

Your broker would much rather have you at the end of a telephone line where you are studying the market than see you in his office listening to tips and gossip.

Very few are really able to trade or invest on their own judgment, but the number is growing. Stock market children who were burned want to know how to avoid the fire.

The small operator has a great advantage in being able to get in and out of the market quickly; the large operator must await a favorable opportunity or create a market that suits him.

The purpose of manipulation is to induce traders to do the opposite to what the manipulator desires to do for himself — make them buy when he wishes to sell and sell when he is buying.

When forming your judgment, all your intellectual powers should be called into play; but when you have reached a decision you should become an order clerk, transmitting to your broker what your judgment dictates.

Why Stop Orders Are Caught

MANY people say: "Whenever I use stop orders they are caught." Which indicates they do not know when to open their trades and where to place their stops. They probably make a practice of buying on bulges. Reactions follow and they are stopped out.

The first step in learning how and when to use stop orders is to learn how and when to go long or short. If you do this correctly, there is little risk of your stop orders being touched off. Learn how to buy and sell scientifically.

When you buy a house you immediately insure yourself against fire. Placing a stop order on a long or short trade is in the same category. The fire policy protects you against a large loss. That is just what the stop order is intended to do.

If your house does not burn, you take a small loss — the premium.

Going long on bulges and selling short on weakness is the equivalent of buying a frame house in the midst of a blazing forest!

Here is the record of fifteen trades made by a student of ours. He placed stop orders ⅛ to ⅝ away on each trade, and moved them according to instructions.

His first one point loss was due to the poor execution of an order. On the other losing trade he put a ⅜ stop when he placed the order, but the trade was made at a price ⅝ above where he expected to get it. When the stop was caught the loss was one point.

								Points *Loss*	Points *Profit*
Feb. 15	Sold short	100	UAF	22⅜	Feb. 20	Cov'd	21⅝....		¾
Feb. 21	" "	100	UAF	22	Feb. 23	"	20⅞....		1⅛
Feb. 21	" "	100	UAF	21⅝	Feb. 23	"	20¾....		⅞
Feb. 21	" "	50	AT&T	98⅞	Feb. 25	"	94⅜....		4½
Feb. 25	" "	50	AT&T	95⅞	Feb. 25	"	94⅜....		1½
Feb. 27	Bought	80	AT&T	94⅜	Feb. 28	Sold	96½....		2⅛
Feb. 28	"	50	AT&T	97½	Mar. 1	"	96½....	1	
Mar. 1	"	100	NPT	11⅛	Mar. 15	"	14¾....		3⅝
Mar. 1	"	100	AT&T	97½	Mar. 15	"	104		6½
Mar. 2	"	100	BOR	18⅞	Mar. 15	"	23		4⅛
Mar. 2	"	100	AM TOB B	53	Mar. 15	"	61¼....		8¼
Mar. 3	"	200	UN CARB	22¼	Mar. 15	"	25⅝....		3⅜
Mar. 16	"	50	UAF	24¾	Mar. 16	"	23¾....	1	
Mar. 17	Sold short	200	UAF	24½	Mar. 17	Cov'd	23		1½
Mar. 20	" "	100	UAF	22⅜	Mar. 21	"	21½....		⅞
					Results of 15 Trades....			2	39⅛

This young man watches the tape throughout the Stock Exchange session, and uses our Tape Reading Charts to supplement what he sees on the tape.

We mention this to prove that trading with close stops *can* be done *with profit* when you know how. And that if stops are rightly placed and moved when the market permits, they are of inestimable value.

Later: The young man has made another and larger series of trades with only one loss of ⅝ of a point.

Never Put Up Cash on a Margin Call

Three Lines of Defense Against Loss

YOUR first line of defense is a stop order — placed when you make the trade, or immediately after.

If you fail to limit your risk at the inception, make a practice of looking over your commitments every day, or twice every week and selling out, at the market, all showing a loss. That will keep your sheet clean and allow your profitable trades to run until the time comes to close them out.

Now suppose that you have ignored these two safeguards and that you still require a third line of defense. You will readily agree that you must have such a third line of defense: otherwise your capital might be swept away in an unexpected stock market move.

What is this third line of defense? It is this: *Never put up cash in response to a margin call.*

When a broker calls you for margin you have final, positive proof that your judgment was wrong when you made the trade. You based it on certain assumptions or facts, tips, rumors, hearsay, statistics, etc., which have not worked out; therefore, you should by this time be convinced that the trades were made at the wrong time, on the wrong side of the market or in the wrong stocks.

Instead of putting up more cash and hanging on to your weak position, confess that you have made a mistake. Tell your broker to close out those losing trades — at once. Take whatever loss you have made and congratulate yourself it is no more, remembering that a loss is punishment for bad judgment.

And thank the broker that he called you for margin because his was the third and last warning that it was time for you to get out.

More Profit in the Swings Than in the Long Pull

ASK the man in Wall Street what he would rather know about the stock market and frequently you will get this answer: "I would like to be able to buy at the bottom and sell at the top."

Now there is much more profit to be had if one can correctly forecast the swings of five points or more. The total of such swings is many more points than the difference between low and high. Furthermore, this buying at the bottom and selling at the top commits you to the bull side. No trader should be so impregnated with the idea that he has to buy first and sell afterwards, because with such an attitude he is only half a trader. He is a one way man.

To get the benefit of these intermediate swings of five to thirty points one must have a certain flexibility in his mental attitude. He must be able and ready to trade on the short side as well as the long. Unless he can do this there is only part of a profit awaiting him in these swings.

Taking up the stock list and selecting the first leading active trading favorite, Allied Chemical, I find that in June, 1932 this stock made a low of $42\frac{1}{2}$. Up to March 23, 1933, nine months later, the high point was $89\frac{7}{8}$. Roughly, the difference between low and high was 47 points.

The record proves that there were 32 swings of five points or more during these nine months. The smallest was five points and the largest twenty-five points. The total of all these swings was 330 points, which is seven times the number of points from low to high. If all these moves of five points or more were added to the low point of $42\frac{1}{2}$ they would make the equivalent of a rise to $372\frac{1}{2}$ which would be something of a bull market in this stock.

The above is of little practical value unless there is a way to forecast and trade on these swings; hence, I now invite your attention to the fact that 75% of these were indicated in advance, to those who understand scientific stock market forecasting.

INTERMEDIATE SWINGS OF FIVE POINTS OR MORE IN ALLIED CHEMI-
CAL FROM JUNE, 1932 TO MARCH 23, 1933

Period			No. Points	Forecastable
June 1932	Advanced from 43 to 61....		18	15
Aug.	Declined	61 to 56....	5	0
	Advanced	56 to 81....	25	25
	Declined	81 to 75....	6	5
	Advanced	75 to 82....	7	5
	Declined	82 to 68....	14	10
	Advanced	68 to 82....	14	9
	Declined	82 to 75....	7	5
	Advanced	75 to 80....	5	4
	Declined	80 to 75.:...	5	4
	Advanced	75 to 86....	11	10
	Declined	86 to 79....	7	6
Sept.	Advanced	79 to 88....	9	5
	Declined	88 to 71....	17	10
	Advanced	71 to 84....	13	11
	Declined	84 to 78....	6	4
	Advanced	78 to 83....	5	3
Sept.–Oct.	Declined	83 to 67....	16	16
Oct.	Advanced	67 to 76....	9	5
	Declined	76 to 69....	7	5
	Advanced	69 to 75....	6	3
Nov.	Declined	75 to 68....	7	4
	Advanced	68 to 82....	14	11
	Declined	82 to 71....	11	11
Dec.	Advanced	71 to 83....	12	10
	Declined	83 to 76....	7	6
Jan. 1933	Advanced	76 to 89....	13	3
Feb.	Declined	89 to 80....	9	7
	Advanced	80 to 85....	5	5
	Declined	85 to 71....	14	14
Mar.	Advanced	71 to 88....	17	10
	Declined	88 to 79....	9	5
			330	246

This tabulation shows that out of 330 points, 246 points could be considered forecastable; that is, the chart formations on these stocks gave evidence in advance, in all but one instance, as to the direction of the moves and the approximate number of points they might extend.

The percentage of accuracy in these forecasts depended upon the ability of the stock market technician making them, but three out of four of the total number of points in 32 swings were discernible in advance by the trained eye.

Don't Lean on Your Broker

FIRST of all it's your money, not your broker's.

If you win it's your profit — not his.

Some people ask their broker's advice before they make a trade so they can blame him if it goes wrong; but they never expect to thank him for any profits he helps them make.

Sixty years ago E. C. Stedman, a member of the New York Stock Exchange, wrote this: "A customer should know his own mind, and have his own opinion, or not deal. It is not the custom to expect a broker to judge the market. If he could always do so, he would not need any customers, but would prefer to deal exclusively for himself."

Gather your own facts; form your own conclusions; make your own decisions; give your own orders. Tell your broker to buy or sell for your account and risk. Don't ask his opinion. He should play no part in your ventures except to execute and finance them.

Scores of people, every day, expect brokers to tell them which stock is best, which way it is going and when to buy or sell. How can the brokers have the right answer always on tap? Such a task is beyond the ability of anyone.

Learn to stand on your own feet marketwise. Then you'll know what to do and what not to do. And you can either blame yourself or pat yourself on the back.

Which is as it should be.

Trading from the Tape

THE information you can derive from the tape and from your charts is far more valuable than any that you can get from any other source. There is an old saying: The tape never lies.

Your judgment should be based on sound premises. You have all the facts before you; assemble these and make your diagnosis. Decide what the situation calls for; then use courage in acting upon your decision. Be courageous, and somewhat bold, but with a certain measure of prudence — alertness and watchfulness combined with caution.

Allow for the unforeseen and the incalculable.

Learn to think and act promptly. Your decision becomes a command to trade. Having placed your order, never fear to revise your opinion. You must have flexibility; the mere holding of a certain position is no *reason* for your holding it; never be bullish or bearish just because you are in a trade.

The market always tells you what to do. It tells you: Get in. Get out. Move your stop. Close out. Stay neutral. Wait for a better chance. All these things the market is continually impressing upon you, and you must get into the frame of mind where you are in reality taking your orders from the action of the market itself — from the tape.

Your judgment will become poorer from the very time when you decide that you know more about the market than the market is telling you. From that moment your results will be unsatisfactory, for in this trading business the tape is the boss. You must learn to obey its orders, doing exactly what it tells you. When you can accomplish this, you are on the high road to success in your stock trading.

"I am not interested in a ten per cent return. I want something that will grow."

— *Edward H. Harriman.*

The Technician Debates with the Fundamentalist

TECH.: For many years now you have been following these fundamental statistics and I would like to inquire how you have made out. Have you really made any big money in the last twenty years?

FUND.: I have not done as well as I expected. I have made quite a pile of money at different times, but there have been other quite extended periods when I found myself on the wrong side of the market, hanging on to a lot of long stocks. I haven't been very much of an operator on the short side.

TECH.: Then your long suit has been to buy for a long pull when you thought conditions were right?

FUND.: Yes, I have always been willing to hold stocks when their earnings were good and the dividends seemed well secured with prospects of higher rates being paid. I admit that these statistics have fooled me many times and kept me from getting out when I should have.

TECH.: Have you ever taken the precaution to limit your risk on any of these commitments?

FUND.: No. I made a practice of holding my long positions based on the above facts until I observed that earnings were falling off; then, I thought, it was time enough to get out.

Statistics are the dust they blow into our eyes while they cut the buttons off our coats

TECH.: But didn't the market often decline seriously without any material change in the earnings and other statistics on which you based your trades?

FUND.: Yes. I did not perhaps turn quickly enough, and I was often disconcerted by the apparently unexplained declines in stocks. It seemed to me that insiders who had been selling must have known that these changes in earnings were coming and based their market commitments accordingly, because there always seemed to have been some wise selling before the declines began.

TECH.: What do you regard as your most reliable indicator among the various factors that you employ?

FUND.: Car Loadings, Commodity Prices, Steel Earnings, Motor Car Production, Electric Power Consumption — these are probably the most valuable.

TECH.: But none of these tell you just when or what to buy or sell, do they?

FUND.: No, I can't say that they do, but I use them as a basis for my calculations as to the broad moves of the market and the probability of turning points being foreshadowed.

TECH.: Do you ever feel the necessity for a more accurate barometer? I mean one that would tell you within a day or two of the actual turning point?

FUND.: Yes. I have never been able to determine turning points so closely, because the changes in the trend of important statistics are slow, requiring weeks or months in their formation of definite indications, under my way of calculating.

TECH.: Why don't you consider the action of the market, that is, the study of supply and demand of stocks as an indicator, instead of all these (what I call) vague and misleading factors which are so difficult to turn to practical account? And why don't you realize that the up-to-date manifestations of supply and demand represent the resultant of all these other forces, including not only those that are observable but many big obscure forces that are not available to the public and sometimes are not even known to the real insiders in the market? All the important factors, both known and unknown, are integrated in this constant readjustment of supply and demand. For instance, three months after the close of the 1932 calendar year I get a report that U. S. Steel Corporation's net income shows a deficit of $71,000,000 for that period. Am I to assume from this that as this report is very bad I am to throw over any Steel common or preferred that I may possess? There seems no other course if I am to act as you do — on fundamental statistics. Certainly there is no indication in those figures that it is time to buy. If, on the other hand, I study the action of Steel common and preferred in the market for the past three or four months, what do I find? Certainly no evidence of approaching calamity. The action of these stocks contradicts the big deficit. The latter says: "Get out," whereas the action of the stock indicates to me that there is something more promising for the future. If I have to wait until the earnings show definite improvement the chances are I will miss the first twenty or thirty points of the rise. But my buying indications will appear when the insiders, who are able to estimate the earnings several months in advance, begin to make their commitments and their banking allies do the same. This will show me, in the face of adverse reports, that it is time to buy. And if I watch these indications on the tape and on my charts I will see them confirmed. As the science of trading requires foresight, we must read the first indications that are available. These are found in the action of stocks and not in statistics covering the general situation or in this company's operations. They don't come along till months after the party is over.

FUND.: What you say certainly deserves consideration.

The Best Stock

For Every Purse, Purpose and Personality

SEND us one dollar and we'll name the stock you really should have. Or, better still, come in and have it fitted to you. What? You haven't a dollar? Well then, here's the list anyhow. Just choose yours from those below. After you have bought it, any broker will tell you it is either going up or going down. For 23 cents additional we furnish footwarmer and lap robe; but as all these issues are rated Ah-h-h by Moody, why worry about cold feet?

For Standing Committees.................Am. Seating
For Blowhards..........................Am. Snuff
For Gossips............................Tel. & Tel.
For Ship Captains......................Anchor Cap.
For Professors.........................Atlas Tack
For Florists...........................Budd
For Wets...............................Canada Dry
For Early Birds........................Caterpillar
For Bankrupts..........................Commercial Credit
For Addicts............................Drug
For Drunkards..........................Gen. Am. Tank
For Firemen............................Combustion
For Traders............................Buy Loew, Sell Loft
For Tightwads..........................Loose Wiles
For Gamblers...........................Kitty pfd.
For Bandits............................Cash Register
For A Sure Rise........................Otis Elevator
For Pikers.............................Penney
For Letter Carriers....................Postal Tel.
For a quiet evening....................Reading
For The Queen of Holland...............Royal Dutch
For Motorists..........................Superior Oil
For High Fliers........................United Aircraft
For Swindlers..........................Gypsum

Alibi: While the above statements are not guaranteed, you can bet your entire margin these are derived from sources that are perfectly ridiculous.

Banker a Bear on Charts

NOT long ago a New York newspaper printed the
following:

> One leading banker deplores the growing use of charts
> by professional stock traders and customers' men, who, he
> says, are causing unwarranted market declines by purely
> mechanical interpretation of a meaningless set of lines. It is
> impossible, he contends, to figure values by plotting prices
> actually based on supply and demand; but, he adds, if too
> many persons play with the same set of charts, they tend to
> create the very unbalanced supply and demand which upsets
> market trends. In his opinion, all charts should be confiscated,
> piled at the intersection of Broad and Wall and burned with
> much shouting and rejoicing.

This banker evidently knows nothing of the real value of
stock charts, nor that judgment must be used in their
interpretation.

It may be however that he makes use of certain charts
himself. Over his desk there probably pass many statistical
services, barometers and other graphic presentations of financial, business and stock market conditions. He probably forms
his opinion from these so-called indicators. We wonder if his
interpretation of such charts is purely mechanical.

He says it is impossible to figure values by plotting prices
actually based on supply and demand. Of course it is!
Chart operators pay no attention to values, if by this he
means earning power, financial position, etc.; they base
trades on their judgment of supply and demand, and, believe me, those who really understand how to trade in this
way are far more successful than bankers and others who
do not.

The banker is worried that "too many persons trading
with the same set of charts will tend to create the very
unbalanced supply and demand which upsets market
trends." Supply and demand are practically always un-

balanced. That is what makes trends. The real cause of his worry, however, is that the public may learn something about the game by the use of charts. As this tendency develops, the banker and his friends, insiders who organize pools and juggle other people's money in their own stock market operations will be less successful. The public now shows a strong desire to learn how to trade successfully, and nothing the banker and his associates can do or print will interfere with that trend.

If and when all charts are confiscated and burned, we presume it will include the banker's own charts. The shouting and rejoicing will be entirely on his side; for the public, after a moment with thumbs to noses, will resume and extend its study of the tape and the charts. The burning ceremony would supply the final and most convincing testimony as to their value.

An economist is said to be a man *who knows* a *great deal* about a *very little;* and who goes along knowing *more and more* about *less and less* until, finally, he knows *practically everything* about *nothing.*

Now a financial fundamentalist, on the other hand, is a man who knows a *very little* about a *great deal,* and keeps on knowing *less and less* about *more and more,* until, finally he knows *practically nothing* about *everything.*

Advantages of a Neutral Position

NO ONE but a floor trader should always be in the market. Those who trade from the tape in an office should assume a neutral position frequently. They should not delude themselves that they can anticipate everything that happens in their favorite stocks. They should take vacations from the tape varying from a walk around the block to a trip into the country for a week or two.

A neutral position clarifies the mind.

Trading should never become a habit (like smoking cigarettes) so that you've simply got to satisfy that craving to jump in and out. Such a practice warps the judgment; eagerness to trade supplants deliberation.

Not because we itch to buy or sell should we make a trade, but because the market says: Here is a real opportunity.

And when we get in, we should not be on a nervous edge until we get out again. When we do this it is because we are not sure of our ground. We should make certain before we start. And only get out because the action of the market indicates it is time to close the trade.

Continually the market is confirming or contradicting what it has previously forecasted. When it fails to do either, we have the sign of a neutral position and we should close out and stand pat until indications again become positive.

It is true that there may be times when a neutral position may lose an opportunity; but there are plenty of other opportunities coming along daily and weekly.

Without any stocks, we are in a far better mental attitude and can judge what it is best to do next. With no open trades we see clearly. We realize perhaps that when we were in that last venture we were bearish because we were short. That is not a good reason; it leads to unnecessary losses.

We should make commitments only when all signs point to a probable profit. Our decisions should be made calmly and deliberately — not under stress or in haste as though this were our last chance to trade.

And so, whenever we feel these elements of uncertainty, either in our conclusions or in the positions we hold, let us clean house and become observers until, as that eminent trader Dickson G. Watts wrote, "The mind is clear; the judgment trustworthy."

The Old Timer Says:

ALL this talk about the market getting away from us amuses me. That expression means: they did not get aboard before the train started — before the current move.

The market really never gets away from us if we are smart. We must continually judge it correctly and act on our judgment promptly.

I don't care whether the market goes up or down. All I want is a piece out of the middle of the principal moves. I don't expect to hit the exact tops or bottoms. The worst thing the market can do from my standpoint is to stand still, so I can't scalp for points.

* * *

When any one tells you that *no one* can forecast the short or the intermediate movements in the stock market with any degree of success, he is merely confessing his own inability to do this. At one time, you recall, people said carriages must have horses hitched to them or they would not go.

The few who have devoted their lives to the science of the stock market have found that accurate and profitable forecasting and trading *can* be done, *has* been done, *is being done* and *will be done.*

When you give a fellow an inside tip on the market, and inform him that he's not to tell another soul, he's going to let at least three or four others in on the secret. And the thing spreads like a fire in the woods. — *Daniel Drew.*

Philosophy of Famous Operators

IF you want to make money in stocks, kill your losses. — *E. H. Harriman.*

* * *

If you can be right three times out of five, and close out quickly when you are wrong, you'll make money. — *James R. Keene.*

* * *

"When you have a good opportunity, get it at once, don't delay, get it while you can; the poor house is full of people who waited and thought it over, or consulted their friends, the banks or the lawyer. Use your own brains with your surplus money and put it to work for you." — *John D. Rockefeller.*

* * *

Whenever Jim Patton found himself wrong he could run out of the market like a scared rabbit. That was one of the reasons he was successful. He knew he could not make a market go his way by being stubborn. . . . I should have had to be pretty dull not to discover that the way to make money was to be as quick as possible in taking a loss, but to be slow in taking profits; rather, to let these pile up as high as they would go. — *Arthur W. Cutten* in Saturday Evening Post.

* * *

It is not the original operator for a rise who always boosts his own stock or commodity. You may wish to put a stock up to eighty, and when it gets to seventy-eight you sometimes find that you have accumulated a lot of followers. In the usual operation for a rise, it is customary to cause a temporary decline to shake out these followers, because they may sell at the wrong time and cause an embarrassing situation. Your followers in Wall Street often cause you more trouble than your opponents. — *Jay Gould.*

Letters from Our Readers

To the Editor:

Two years ago I entered a book store in Helsingfors, Finland, with the intention of buying an English novel, in order to get some training in your language. I came out with a copy of your book "Wall Street Ventures and Adventures through Forty years."

Your introduction fascinated me, and I read further, without interruption, until I came to page 179, where you say: "If I were beginning my Wall Street career now, and knew what forty years of it have taught me, I should apply myself first of all to this business of judging and forecasting the stock market by its own action." Here I stopped reading, underlined this sentence with a blue pencil, and decided to follow your advice.

I had had some sad experiences on the Helsingfors Stock Exchange; when I had finished your book I saw very clearly which errors I had made, and I knew how to find the right road.

In 1930 I had published, except my doctor's thesis, three investigations in the field of physiological chemistry, which attracted some attention. In the spring of 1931 a large research organization informed me that they would like to have me continue this work at any laboratory I chose, and that they would pay my expenses plus a stipend for one year. My wish to study the American stock market at a closer range was a major factor when I decided to come to the United States.

The first thing I did after my arrival in this country was to order a number of books and daily stock charts for fifty stocks from 1926 to date. Over these charts I spent four to five hours every night, making imaginary trades as I gradually uncovered a chart, or studying them in conjunction with the financial news in old newspapers and magazines. When I had a fair idea of the game I began to trade on paper. After a few months I had the satisfaction of being right more often than wrong, and consequently began to buy and sell actual shares, outright, through my bank. This trading has resulted in a fair profit.

Having completed my chemical investigations here, I returned to Finland, but realized soon how restricted the opportunities in Europe are in comparison to those offered in the United States. The Helsingfors market is so thin that stop loss orders won't give an adequate protection, and no short sales are permitted there. So I came to New York last December.

Some time ago I noticed your signature on the title page of a copy of "Stock Market Technique," which I immediately bought. I was very glad to learn that you are back in Wall Street, and that you are carrying out the plan you mentioned at the end of your book, namely to make available to others more of the rich store of knowledge which you have accumulated, and of the methods which you have created. I trust that it sometime will be possible for me to avail myself of your Course of Instruction in Stock Trading, not only because I know its great value, but also because I then may have a chance of meeting the man who has shown me the way.

Having attained a 55–60% accuracy in forecasting the intermediate swings, I will now concentrate on Tape Reading. The influence of time, volume, etc., are probably essentially the same as by the intermediate swings, so I trust that I will be able to arrive to an accuracy of 55% in Tape Reading within a year or so.

I have written this letter to you, Mr. Wyckoff, because I thought it might interest you, as a pioneer and a teacher, to know how far beyond the geographical limits of the United States your influence is extending, and how your book has changed the life and prospects of a young man living on the distant shores of Finland.

I also wish to express my best thanks to you, not only because your book revived my interest in stock trading when I was about to give up the game as a hopeless one, but particularly because you have shown me the path, which we know will lead to success.

With the best wishes for further success and satisfaction in the continuation of your work,

Yours very sincerely,

J—— B——

To the Editor:

The investor, according to the orthodox definition, is one who buys securities for safety and income, in the belief that his interest or dividends will continue for a considerable period and be amply secured by earnings. He is usually satisfied to make his purchases, then "put them away and forget them," until some day when he is notified that his dividends are being cut or passed. Then he begins to look into the situation and considers the advisability of disposing of such holdings. He may recall that since he purchased them they may have had substantial rises but that subsequently they have declined and now show him a loss. In general he pays little consideration to the question of disposing of anything until something goes wrong with it.

Many men claim to have made considerable money as investors. Close investigation of their records generally show that they have not been investors but traders, because they have been alert to consider developments which indicated when it was time to dispose of holdings originally bought as investments.

The real profits are secured by those who assume a trading attitude and know when to sell as well as when to buy. The trader observes conditions which show him when it is time to act. The investor, on the other hand, does not usually give a thought to his position until a situation develops that is so bad that manifestly it must have been discounted long before the event by a substantial decline in price.

In view of these considerations I would prefer to be a trader rather than an investor.   W. L. J.

*   *   *

An out-of-town broker writes: "I get more out of your writings that relate to judging the market from the tape than from all the other sources of so-called information. My people call me up and say they have some great information from New York and give me orders to buy this or that stock. I tell them the action of the stock indicates it is going lower, but that seems to make no difference; the big tip from a New York bank or someone 'supposed to know' is what seems to get them. They get in and lose their money.

"I often ask clients why they watch the tape if they don't understand how to read it. 'I'll tell you,' said one of them, 'we just sit, look and hope.'"

*   *   *

If you plan to speculate in stocks, it behooves you to ask yourself if you possess the temperament and the swift and accurate reasoning powers necessary to cope with the ablest money getters in the world. If you do, you will find that hardly a day passes in which you are not offered opportunities to prove your skill in money making.

Editorial

I CLAIM that it is now practically impossible for any man or organization to absorb, analyze and digest the many so-called fundamental factors which influence the course of the stock market, and deduce therefrom a conclusion from which the course of prices may be predicted with any fair percentage of success; what is more, it is a fallacy to believe this can be done on that basis. All the elements which have gone to produce the lines on the fundamental charts have already been discounted in the market.

It is generally true that those who work on the above basis ignore the highly important factor of stock market technique, which includes, as its main element, a study of the supply and demand plus the manipulative forces that are constantly at work in practically all of the active stocks.

If any one believes he can, more or less continuously, from the so-called fundamental factors alone, predict movements of ten to thirty points in the average prices of any standard group of stocks, I should like very much to know his name, for I have been searching for him for many years.

Numerous people have claimed that they could do this, but I have not found any one who could; nor have I encountered, after a careful search, any one who is well satisfied with the results obtained from operations conducted on the basis of fundamentals alone, wholly ignoring technical factors.

* * *

Brilliant remarks by the otherwise well-informed Samuel Untermyer: "Floor traders are the most pernicious of all short sellers. Short selling is gambling pure and simple."

Will the eminent Samuel explain why the man who sells before he buys is either pernicious or a gambler? Does not he, Untermyer, accept retainers for agreements he has not drawn? That is short selling. He covers when he delivers the completed papers.

A GREAT DEAL OF TALENT is lost in the world for want of a little courage. Every day sends to their graves obscure men whom timidity prevented from making a first effort; who, if they could have been induced to begin, would in all probability have gone great lengths in the career of fame. The fact is, that to do anything in the world worth doing, we must not stand back shivering and thinking of the cold and danger, but jump in and scramble through as well as we can. It will not do to be perpetually calculating risks and adjusting nice changes; it did very well before the Flood, when a man would consult his friends upon an intended publication for a hundred and fifty years, and live to see his success afterwards; but at present, a man waits, and doubts, and consults his brother, and his particular friends, till one day he finds he is sixty-five years old and that he has lost so much time in consulting others that he has no more time to follow their advice.—SYDNEY SMITH.

Greetings

To my Old Friends,
Clients and Subscribers:

In 1926, when a physical breakdown required me to cease all stock market and publishing activities, I resigned as Editor of The Magazine of Wall Street.

Later, in 1928, I disposed of all my Advisory Services, and since then I have not been connected with any financial publishing or advisory business.

Now, after five years spent in regaining my health, I am back in Wall Street once more.

It will be a great pleasure to resume business relations with you.

Cordially yours,

Richard D. Wyckoff

March, 1932